Battlefield Faith

I hoped to survive, I struggled to persevere, I placed my trust in my God and I found Battlefield Faith!

Loudermilk

Copyright © 2018 John Milford Loudermilk
All right reserved
ISBN-9781717977236

Dedication

I dedicate this book to Sandy, the love of my life, and my two wonderful children, Stefanie and Johnny (and Michelle); to my charming grandchildren, Jonathan (and Gey), Grace, Steven, Jared, Jenna, Justin and my precious great-grandson Grayson and to the many great grandsons and granddaughters whom I may never have the privilege to hold in my arms. As you read what I have written here please know you were in my thoughts as I penned the message of this book.

I also dedicate this book to my brothers of the 5th Marines, and especially the 1st Platoon, Charlie Company (1967-1968), Vietnam Veterans. You are some of the bravest, courageous, patriotic men I have ever known.

Table of Contents

Acknowledgements
Preface
Introduction
Chapter 1: My Adventure Begins
Chapter 2: On to the Philippines
Chapter 3: Battle Prepped
Chapter 4: Earning My Salt
Chapter 5: No Steak and Eggs
Chapter 6: Of Swamp and Mines
Chapter 7: Three Walk Away
Chapter 8: A Man's Worth
Chapter 9: Endeavor to Persevere
Chapter 10: The Battle of Hue City
Chapter 11: A Man's Groan, A Baby's Cry
Chapter 12: Heavy Hands and Heart
Chapter 13: Hanging In There
Chapter 14: Home Sweet Home
Conclusion
Addendum
About John Loudermilk 1

Acknowledgements

First and foremost I want to thank my Lord and Savior, Jesus Christ, for His comforting presence during the time I spent in combat as a U.S. Navy corpsman assigned to the 5th Marines of the 1st Marine Division in Vietnam during 1967-1968. The Lord was with me every moment of every night and every day. I have witnessed miracles wrought by prayer and faith in a God who hears us when we pray.

I want to thank my Mother and Father, Jean and Luther Loudermilk; my brothers and sister, Robert, Don and Ruth; my Pastor, Reverend W.C. Edgel and his wife Irene; my grandmother, Joie Nunley, my grandfather, John Hudson Nunley and my wonderful church family at the Hatmaker Street Church of God in Cincinnati, Ohio. I am here today and able to bear witness of the evidence of your faith and prayers in the words of this book.

I want to thank Lieutenant Nick Warr and Staff Sergeant John Mullan for their leadership. I want to thank all of the Marines of 1st Platoon, Charlie Company 1st Battalion, 5th Marines of 1967-1968 with whom I personally endured the challenges of combat. I want to especially thank those Marines who watched my back as I went about my duties as corpsman.

I thank you LORD. I thank you family. I thank you friends. I thank you Marines.

Psalms 46:1-7 *God is our refuge and strength, a very present help in trouble. Therefore will not we fear, though the earth be removed, and though the mountains be carried into the midst of the sea; Though the waters thereof roar and be troubled, though the mountains shake with the swelling thereof. Selah.*
There is a river, the streams whereof shall make glad the city of God, the holy place of the tabernacles of the most High. God is in the midst of her; she shall not be moved: God shall help her, and that right early. The heathen raged, the kingdoms were moved: he uttered his voice, the earth melted. The LORD of hosts is with us; the God of Jacob is our refuge. Selah. (KJV)

Preface

Revelation 6:3, 4 *And when he had opened the second seal, I heard the second beast say, Come and see. And there went out another horse that was red: and power was given to him that sat thereon to take peace from the earth, and that they should kill one another… (KJV)*

War is a thief! He steals, he kills, and he destroys. I fought in a bitter war and experienced firsthand the devastations of battle. With my fellow warriors I looked directly into the face of the thief, the murderer we call War. But I never felt I was alone; I had an ever present Helper who was always at my side. I surrendered my will to God's will as a teen and I knew in whatever circumstance I found myself I would find solace in His Word and presence. I felt as long as I placed my trust in God he would always be at my side. He would always be near, only a prayer away. He was not some strange being that I had to memorize verses or go through some ritual to reach but He became my Friend, my Confidant, and my Personal Savior. I talked to him like I would my best friend and He was. What a Friend I found in Jesus those many dark, wet, dreary nights on ambush and those uncertain days walking through the jungles and rice paddies of Vietnam on patrol with the Marines. God was with me as my helicopter laden with men and arms flew bravely into hostile enemy hideaways and the Spirit of God walked before and beside me as we ventured into the thick bush to seek out the infiltrator who had come to steal and to kill.

God helped me to gain the wisdom, knowledge and understanding that I needed so that I would be able to serve those men who were placed in my care. He guided my hand as I dressed the horrible wounds War had inflicted on my fellow Marines. He was with me and the two other corpsmen when we delivered a tiny baby girl in the heat of the Battle of Hue City in February of 1968 during the Tet Offensive.

Battlefield Faith

I went to war because I had volunteered to be of service to the country I love. I placed my confidence in the men who had been given authority over me but I placed my supreme trust in the God whom I felt was a very present help. I was privileged when the U. S. Navy assigned me to the Fifth Marine Regiment. I was further honored when I was billeted to the First Platoon of Charlie Company. I am proud to say I have served with some of the bravest and most valiant men I have ever known.

On the following pages I want to share a most significant part of my life. I've heard it said that some people excel or reach their peak at different times in their life. I often thought, "Did I reach my plateau at age 20"? Frequently when I would dwell on this idea I would become somewhat depressed and wondered if I would ever amount to anything. But as I have grown a little older and hopefully a little wiser I look back at a few of these moments in my life and realize that some things do happen early on but they tend to become resources one can draw from later in life.

It has taken me a very long time to get started on this writing. I have made notes over the years and have put them away thinking I would never get back to them. But here I am reminiscing again. I have discovered that many of my memories and feelings have been hidden. Like so many other combat veterans I have problems remembering names and the faces of the incredible young men I served with and we all have changed so much that I wouldn't know my dearest friends if we should meet and I am confident they wouldn't know me.

I want to share some very personal letters. These are my thoughts and requests for prayer for God's Divine protection when I was in battle. Like my friend, Harold Thrasher, wrote in his book (Suicide Charlie, Brothers Never Forgotten) that he believed he is here because of Divine Intervention. I too am a believer that GOD in HIS infinite wisdom had a reason for blessing me and allowing me to return to my loved ones who so earnestly held my name up in prayer through those trying times.

There were instances when in the heat of battle many of our Marines were wounded severely and I often felt so overwhelmed with my duties that I cried, Oh, GOD! And I believe God heard me. Often when faced with so many traumatic injuries at once I felt it was more than I could bear but somehow I reached deep into my resolve and by faith and the grace of God did my best to save as many as I could of those brave young men.

My earnest objective in writing this book was for it to be a source of strength and inspiration for anyone suffering from PTSD especially the combat veteran and for those men and women who may be facing or engaged in combat. My hope is that someone may find comfort in seeing how my faith in God sustained me before, during and after my compelling battlefield experiences. I have inserted scriptures that I feel relate to these incidents and hope you find them uplifting. I could not have endured the challenging events that I personally faced without my faith in my "Personal" Savior, Jesus Christ.

The greatest thing that sustained me during these vexing times was my Battlefield Faith in God! You may feel like giving in or giving up but God never gives up on you!

Mark 11:22 *And Jesus answering saith unto them, Have faith in God.*
Hebrews 11:1 *Now faith is the substance of things hoped for, the evidence of things not seen.*
(KJV)

Introduction

I was born in Williamsburg (Whitley County), Kentucky just a short distance from the Kentucky/Tennessee line. My Dad was a coal miner and farmer during his younger years. Mother was the daughter of a coal miner. She grew up in a Kentucky mining camp. These camps were once a lifestyle of many Americans. They were self-sufficient. The miners were paid with "script" and then the family would spend it at the company store. My Mother and Dad were loving and very hard working parents. They taught us to believe and trust in God from an early age.

At one point in my young life Mother and Dad were trying to make the move to Cincinnati, Ohio where my Dad would be able to get a better job. He had to leave us during the week but came home on the weekends. Mother was left to tend to us alone while he was gone. We didn't have a telephone but we had good neighbors who looked after one another. I remember an elderly gentleman by the name of Mr. Paris Owens who lived just across the road from us at one point. He kept an eye on us when Dad was gone. There was a "rolling store" in those days which was a large truck from a grocer in town that made its way to the outlying areas where much of the community lived. We always looked forward to seeing the welcome site of that truck stopping at our place.

Like most country folks we didn't have a television so when evening drew nigh Mother would get her very large Bible Story Book down and read an inspiring adventure from God's Word. I thought the stories were fascinating and we all listened intently as Mother read. She told us of Samson who was anointed of God and had great strength when the Spirit of God was upon him. We learned how Samson fought many battles for his God and his nation. We heard of Noah and his obedience to God and how the flood came and Noah and his family were safe upon the Ark that God had shown him to build. Mother read stories of the prophets, the mouthpieces of God in olden times that interceded for the people and many more. I have never forgotten those times and I feel I have drawn strength from those memories.

Mother with John, squinting, Don, Ruth Ann, Robert around 1954

This is my Dad and me around 1951 or 1952. That 12 gauge shotgun I'm holding was 40 years old when I was born. I still have it.

One memory I have of my childhood is when my brother, Robert, and I got the idea we'd like to have a chicken dinner. We were just scrappy little boys. Mother and Dad had some wonderful chickens. I remember Mother saying that she had a Rhode Island Red which laid double yellow yolks. We began to chase those chickens as they ran in every direction. We fell a few times but got up, dusted ourselves off and started out again. We were just about exhausted when we finally caught one. We didn't realize it at the time but it just happened to be Mother's favorite laying hen. We were so engrossed in our adventure that we didn't stop to think about our actions. So I ran and retrieved the hatchet. We just thought we would take care of business and we'd have a chicken dinner. Robert didn't hesitate and began to hold the chicken snugly as I used the hatchet. When we took it to our Mother to cook she wasn't very happy to say the least. However she did fix us a chicken dinner that evening but we paid for it dearly. We can truthfully say we learned one of life's lessons that day.

My Mother cooked on a coal cooking stove during this time. We lived way out in the country and didn't have the conveniences of city living. I remember that somehow the vent pipe from the stove came loose once and she was unable to use it. Robert and I wondered what we could do to help so we put our heads together and gathered up a few things from around the barn. We found an old metal shelf rack from a refrigerator and a few bricks. We somehow figured out how to make a little grill for her to use. Looking back I think we did pretty well for our ages. Mother was pleased that she could use our grill until Dad could fix the stove when he came home on the weekend.

My Grandpa Nunley, Mother's Dad, had fought in World War 1 as a US Army Soldier. I was proud of him and admired how strong and polished he looked in the picture we have of him in his Army "Doughboy" green. He never talked about the war. I have no memories of any stories he ever shared. I wish I could go back and ask him a few questions. I wish we could have spent more time one on one.

He was a Christian gentleman, a hard worker and a fine example for his family to follow. He had endured many hardships for his country in the trenches of World War I. I always looked up to him. I felt he was proud of me when I visited him and Grandma after I returned home from Vietnam in September of 1968. That meant very much to me. Mother and I drove down from Cincinnati in the 1964 red Triumph Spitfire convertible that I bought with the money I had saved on the books when I left Viet Nam.

Grandpa John Hudson Nunley

At the beginning of 1968 I was fighting for my life and trying my best to save as many lives as I could. Later in the year I came home. The beginning and the ending of the year were complete opposites. 1968 was a tough year and a good year. I'll tell you more about that later but for now here is my story…

Chapter 1

My Adventure Begins

Psalms 71:5 *For thou art my hope, O Lord GOD: thou art my trust from my youth.* (KJV)

My family made the move to Cincinnati and we settled into an area we liked. I met some great friends at our neighborhood church. It was the Hatmaker Street Church of God and we began attending during my early teen years. One of our favorite pastimes on the weekend was to get a bus pass on Sundays and ride the bus all over the Cincinnati area. We'd go to places like the parks, the zoo, and the museums or wherever else we wanted to go. But when I turned sixteen our mode of transportation changed. I was able to get my driver's license and as every young driver knows, that provides you with some liberty. I was able to visit some of my friends who lived a little farther away than I would normally be able to walk. One of them was Chuck Hollis. Chuck was a little younger than me so I used to call him my "little brother."

One of the things my brothers and I used to do was to go and explore the railroad tracks and the banks of the Ohio River near our home. We thought we could usually find some cool stuff that was thrown off the train by the railroad men. Often we would find good 9 volt batteries they had discarded because they were not as strong as they thought they needed to be for their lamps but for us they worked just fine. We would usually find other treasures too.

I recall this particular summer was very hot so we decided to meander down to the river and take a swim. My brothers and I were used to the river current but it was something new to Chuck. We were all having a lot of fun in the water and making so much noise that we took our eyes off of Chuck for a moment. He had straddled a log and the current had started to pull him away from the river bank. When he realized what was happening he jumped off of his ride. Unfortunately he was now in deep water! He began to scream for help. I began to swim toward him immediately as quickly as I could. When I reached him and before I could say anything he haphazardly jumped upon my back and his weight pushed me under water. The only thing I could do was to swim toward the river bank with all my effort. So I swam as fast and as hard as I could. I kept my eyes open so I could see the river bottom with Chuck's hands and arms clinging tightly around my neck. When I felt it was safe to stop swimming and stand up I did just that! We both took a great sign of relief as we stood up. We were so thankful to the good Lord for watching over us and helping us to get to safety and that we would live and be able to swim another day.

When I look back on these times and the fun I had with my friends I realize there were other things happening too. There was a lot of unrest in our country and the world then but I didn't feel like it involved me personally at the time. I hated to watch the news in the evening but I learned about current events each night as my Dad routinely turned the channel on our old black and white television set to its designated station at six pm. That television had the old "rabbit ears" antenna. You didn't have to be a genius to realize tensions were building up in Southeast Asia just by listening at the reports on the screen. We never really worried about the war that was stirring up overseas and quite frankly I don't remember paying much attention to it.

I really didn't have much to worry about at home. My Dad worked hard and paid the bills and kept a roof over our heads, food on the table and clothes on our backs. My Mom kept us clean and fed and lovingly nurtured her family. But looking back at those times I realize many young men were being drafted not long after they graduated from high school and I had a few friends of my own that had volunteered for service. Sometimes I felt like I didn't have much of a choice with my future. I thought I would end up in the military somehow. It was like a shadow hanging over a young man's head during those days. We would see some of our neighbors' sons coming home from boot camp in their new uniforms and they looked so proud. Most of them were teenagers. I soon learned you could join the military at age 17 with your parent's signature, however, one of life's stories I woefully discovered later was that you could join the military, be sent to war where your young life would be in danger at age 18. But after I was on active duty one thing that bothered many of us was the fact that we weren't allowed to vote. We couldn't get credit even though our jobs were secure with no possibility of being laid off. Some of the guys were upset that they couldn't buy alcoholic beverages but that one didn't bother me.

As I mentioned earlier my Grandfather had been a World War I soldier. I had heard the incredible stories of him going off to war. I had two uncles that were Navy Chiefs at the time and I had heard of their adventures and I was eager to launch out on my own. I had a young man's heart that longed for adventure and I knew the only way I would ever see another part of the world would be for me become part of the armed forces. I wanted to find out about the military for myself so I visited several recruiters and got all the reading material I could find from all of them. I thought the Marine Corps had the best looking uniforms. I didn't know which branch to choose but I favored the Navy because of my uncles. People were saying that if you join the Navy at least you would get three meals a day and have a clean bed to sleep in at night. Boy did I find out that one was not true in my case.

(May 11, 1965, Taking the Oath) That's me in the middle in light shirt

I turned seventeen in March of 1965 and then in May I joined the Navy just a few weeks after my seventeenth birthday. I didn't finish high school and that was a mistake but I did complete my studies later in 1967 while stationed in the Philippines. My Mother didn't want me to enlist but my Dad was o.k. with it. It seemed like the days passed quickly after I made my decision and soon I was on my way to the induction center. There were a lot of young men my age there and I felt I had much in common with them. After all of the examinations and the swearing in ceremony I was on my way to the Great Lakes Naval Training Center. I had never been on a plane and this was a new experience for me. I remember all of the people from various walks of life going to so many different places. The flight was exciting but a little challenging for me but all went well and we flew to the Chicago O'Hare airport I believe. I then made my way to the Great Lakes Naval Training Center with the other men.

When we arrived we were ushered into a large open building where the men would practice their drills and exercises. I remember my first day quite well and the very first words I heard at our initial muster (roll call). The Petty Officer in charge addressed us, told us who he was and then said, "I want all of you men to know that this is the worst mistake you have ever made in your life!" Like the other young men just out of high school standing there I thought, "What have I done?" I thought to myself, "I have four years of military service ahead of me. I hope this man is not right. I hope there is something better ahead than what he is telling us."

It turned out I had it pretty easy compared to most recruits in basic training. I had been in the band in High School and played the trumpet pretty well and the Navy Drum and Bugle Corps was taking auditions. I told them I'd like to audition and they sent me to another large building that housed a huge gymnasium. When I walked inside I noticed a stairway and looked up and saw a series of rooms. The sound of a trumpet was echoing throughout the building. I began to think, "I hope I'm good enough." I made my way upstairs and found the audition room. I walked in and was told to have a seat and wait my turn. When it was finally my turn to try out the Petty Officer in charge handed me a trumpet and asked me to play something I had played in high school. I chose an Al Hirt tune I had learned and enjoyed playing and when I finished he looked at me and said, "You're in." I was very excited. This membership in the Great Lakes Naval Station Drum and Bugle Corps would afford me the great opportunity to be able to go off base during my boot camp training days for parades around Illinois. I would be able to get away from the rigors of training and escape maybe for just a little while but any time away would be good. I would be able to see some new sights. Our Corps represented the Naval Training Center proudly wherever we went and we were well liked in all the small towns we visited.

I did have the usual Navy boot camp training however and after taking a battery of tests they asked me what I wanted to do. I said, "I think I'd like to be a radioman." The Petty Officer replied, "That's great, you're going to be a hospital corpsman." I had no idea what that was at the time but I figured I must have scored high on the required courses for that job.

We were given a couple of weeks leave to go home after we graduated from boot camp and I received my orders to Hospital Corps School which wasn't far from the boot camp area. I was very fortunate in getting what the Navy calls an A school because at the time I was not a high school graduate. I can't remember how many weeks I was at Corps School but some of the courses I remember were: first aid, patient care, anatomy & physiology, drug classifications and toxicology and preventative medicine. At the end of the classroom studies we had our first required hospital ward training at the Great Lakes Naval Hospital. I remember being amazed at the large number of wounded Marines in the hospital wards. I didn't know much about what was going on in Southeast Asia at that time.

Somewhere around late 1965 I graduated from Hospital Corps School and received my new orders to the Portsmouth, Virginia Naval Hospital which was pretty close to Norfolk, Virginia. Every corpsman had to serve six months of hospital ward duty training upon graduation and Portsmouth is where I was sent to do mine.

I remember my first day at my new duty station. After reporting in and putting my gear away I recall sitting on my bunk and realizing I didn't know a soul. I felt so all alone. That first weekend seemed to drag on forever. I began thinking I had a long time ahead of me before I could go home again. I didn't know what my future held. With no one else to turn to, with no friend near to comfort me I relied on my faith in God.

Deuteronomy 31:8 *And the LORD, he it is that doth go before thee; he will be with thee, he will not fail thee, neither forsake thee: fear not, neither be dismayed.* (KJV)

My solitude didn't last very long because when Monday morning rolled around I met the crew I would be working with and we stayed very busy. We cared for a lot of wounded Marines here also who had returned from 'Nam. I met some wonderful guys. Some of them called me "Johnny Cool". Others called me "Buttermilk". I was just a 17 year old kid right out of high school and now I found myself on active duty as a member of our nation's armed forces. I remember thinking, "this is for real". I had a lot of responsibility for my age and the nurses and senior corpsman kept an earnest eye on all of us new men. I was assisting nurses and doctors in their daily tasks and adding to my medical knowledge every day.

Loudermilk

Most weekends when I was off duty were very boring. I didn't have much to do. I never made much money as a junior enlisted man so my adventures were very limited. I didn't have a car and I didn't really know how to get around. I was in a new environment and only felt comfortable on base. This was my first real time away from home. The Commanding Officer had established a radius that clearly showed our limited boundary for the weekends. They didn't want any of us to venture too far after hours on our liberty. But as I reached the end of my 6 months tour of duty I just had to take a chance and go home for a day or two. I didn't know if I was going to get another leave before I shipped out or not and I had no idea of where my next duty station would be. It just happened that another corpsman from Ohio was in the same predicament as me but he had a car and he said he'd give me a ride as far as Columbus then I could hitch a ride on to Cincinnati. It sounded like a great idea to me at the time so we went for it. I was young and this was just another adventure to me. At seventeen you don't think much about negative consequences.

We waited until we both had a weekend off and then we left after work on Friday evening and drove to Columbus quickly without incident. My friend dropped me off as we planned and we agreed where and when he would pick me up. We went over our agreement of the times and places so we both knew exactly what we were going to do. I assured him I would be there promptly. I was able to hitchhike some rides to Cincinnati pretty easily after I saw my friend drive away.

I remember having a great weekend at home. We enjoyed our family time at home and I was able to attend church with my family and friends on Sunday Morning. I was thankful for just being with my family again if only for a short time. However, it seemed like I had just gotten home when it was time for me to head back to Virginia. The weekend whizzed by like a dream. It wasn't long until I was on my way back to Portsmouth. My Dad and Mother didn't want me to hitchhike so they said they would take me as far as Columbus where I was supposed to meet my friend.

Our car was old. It was a six cylinder with a stick shift transmission and both the engine and transmission seemed to wind out tight at 60 miles per hour. We made it most of the way but our 1956 Ford broke down on I75 somewhere between Cincinnati and Columbus and I had to get a ride. As much as I regretted to leave them stranded I had to say goodbye to my family and continue on. They assured me it was alright and told me I must go. A guy in a Chevy Corvair stopped to see if we needed any help as we were talking and said he would take me to the edge of Columbus. I was wearing my Navy dress white uniform at the time. I thought it might help me get a ride in case this very thing happened. Well, I was right. The man dropped me off somewhere in Columbus and I then walked to the curb and put out my thumb. It wasn't long until a High School girl and her older sister in a 1966 Mustang Fastback picked me up and took me across the city to the place where I was supposed to meet my ride to the base. I thought they had a beautiful car. While driving they asked me all about the Navy of which I knew very little at the time but I tried my best to answer their questions. I think they enjoyed giving a sailor a ride in their new car. I guess it gave them something to talk about when they went back to their routines on Monday. They dropped me off, wished me luck and said goodbye and I began to look for my friend at our designated meeting place.

    I waited and waited but he didn't show up. I thought it was getting late. This was Sunday and I got a little uneasy thinking I would not make it back in time for muster on Monday morning and I didn't want to get into any trouble. I didn't want to start my career out with a bad entry on my record so I stuck out my thumb again. I quickly caught another ride. They took me a little farther but dropped me off on the expressway and exited. There I stood on the side of that Ohio highway. I felt like I was in the middle of nowhere and again, all alone as the traffic sped by. I didn't really know where I was. I just continued to follow the route I had in my mind. I knew I had to head toward Pennsylvania and then veer south toward Virginia somehow.

    I walked for a while and all kinds of thoughts ran through my mind. I thought of home, my family, and my friends I had just left and the wonderful short weekend we had together. I walked on as I daydreamed. It wasn't too long until I saw a sort of fork in the highway and I wasn't sure of which way to go. Not many cars were passing by and it was getting late. It wouldn't be long until the sun would be going down and I'd be out there all by myself with just the night birds and speeding cars for company and now they couldn't see me.

    I started to feel a little uneasy. Not too many cars were passing me by now. But then I heard a vehicle in the distance. He drew nearer and nearer. He seemed to be slowing down somewhat. I thought, "Maybe he sees me?" I wasn't sure of my exact position so I got the idea that I would flag them down just to ask for directions. As they drew nearer I realized it was a pickup truck and on the bed it looked like it had a cattle rack attached. When they saw me wave they slowed to a stop. I then looked and saw a man and a woman inside. They were several years older than me. As we began our conversation I thought they seemed very friendly. The man was wearing a type of western hat and the woman wore a scarf which was fashionable in the sixties. I told him I only needed directions and asked if they could help me. We talked for a while through their opened window then they opened their door and invited me in to ride. As we began driving down the road they told me they had just come from a Louis Armstrong Concert and were headed home. I explained about my ride not showing up on our agreed upon time and we continued on. The woman said she saw me first and told her husband it looked like I was waving for help or wanted to ask for directions. Her husband said he knew I would need a ride. They took me a pretty good distance and we had a great conversation but it was time for me to get out because they were going in a different direction than I was. I enjoyed their friendship and the gift of their ride which got me a little closer to my destination. We said our good byes and I found myself on the side of the road again.

Here I was, alone and not really knowing which way to go. I had no map. We didn't have cell phones in the 60s. As the evening shadows began to form I said a short prayer for comfort and direction and I remembered:

Psalms 119:105 ... *Thy word is a lamp unto my feet, and a light unto my path.* (KJV)

So I thought, "I must continue on!" I was hoping and praying someone would stop and offer me a ride. I was feeling very desperate by this time. The way seemed far and the journey tough and so I continued on.

I think I was going through Pennsylvania now and I felt I was getting closer to Virginia. I walked a quite a ways before I got another ride. I began to hear the sound of the night birds and chirping of the crickets in the brush. Some cars passed but no one offered to pick me up. I couldn't blame them. It was getting dark. But I was surely looking for another ride. Then I saw a newer car coming. It was a 1965 Chevy Impala. It was only a few months old. As they drew nearer I saw two guys, one white, one black, about my age in the front seat. They looked over; I motioned and they stopped for me. They were dressed in civilian clothes but said they were both in the Navy and they were coming from Cincinnati and were heading to a ship home ported in Norfolk which was just across the bay from my duty station in Portsmouth. They said they would give me a ride if I would pay for the gas. I had a little money so I agreed. I thought that surely was a nice car. The driver said he had not had it long. I remember riding in the back seat looking over the front seat at the beautiful new dash with its pretty lights as we drove along. It even had some kind of an engine vacuum gauge and a tachometer. I thought, "I wish my family had a car this nice". I felt badly leaving them stranded on the side of the road in Ohio. I don't know how they all got back home but God blesses those he possesses. We made good time to Portsmouth and they dropped me off pretty close to my barracks. I thanked them for the ride and they drove away. I never saw them again but I have never forgotten them or that cool '65 Chevy Impala.

    I made it back in plenty of time and even caught a few winks before I had to start my day on Monday morning. The fellow that was supposed to pick me up in Columbus didn't have such luck. It seems he was late getting started and didn't get back to the base on time. He got into some trouble and gave them my name and said I had been with him. This little escapade went down in my Naval Record as a strike against me. The Navy made it real official and said I had broken an Article in the Uniformed Code of Military Justice. Oh, well, like I said I was 17. I don't think I had been in the Navy more than a year and I had a lot to learn. I thought to myself at least I made it back on time and I reported for duty "on time" in a spic and span uniform, shined shoes and fresh haircut and finished my Monday without any consequence but most of all I had been able to see my family before I would be shipped out.

    After that escapade I began to focus more on learning my job and caring for the wounded Marines we tended to daily. Most of them had severe injuries that required continuous 24 hour attention. The corpsman and Nurses had set schedules. We had shifts and duty. Your shift is your daily work assignment. Your duty was a job you did after hours and it was in addition to your daily work. We rotated from days to nights. There was always someone on duty. We worked shifts because we had to be at our best when we were on duty. Lives would depend on it. We were attentive. We were efficient. We were caring. We were young but we were adaptable and we took our work very seriously. We had great teachers and we were gaining some of the necessary experience we would need in our near future.

Loudermilk

Every once in a while the USO would put together a show for our patients. Once a country band came to visit and their guitar player had some car trouble and was going to be late. The Sailors and Marines yelled, "Get Buttermilk!" He can play guitar. That's what they called me here. I could play a little but I didn't feel I could play well enough to sit in with this band. I can't remember how well I did but I do remember they were some great guys and friendly. We had a magician there too. He was an elderly gentleman and he was great. He told me to be a magician you must learn to do hand gestures like a female. He had a great act. He was also one of our patients. He was a retired serviceman and had slipped on a cube of ice and became injured. He had gotten well enough to be part of the show.

One of the greatest thrills of a young man's life was seeing a movie star in person and here she was: Joie Lansing in person! She was a very beautiful and popular movie star in the '60s. She came with her entourage one weekend and visited all of the patients on our ward. All the guys loved her and she showed her respect and love for the sacrifices they were making. I'll always remember how caring she seemed.

As the days passed at Portsmouth I acquired more experience and learned much about my responsibilities as a Navy Hospital corpsman. I gained considerable respect for these Marines who had volunteered, suffered and sacrificed for the country they loved. I met some unselfish young men from all walks of life.

Chapter 2

On to the Philippines

It wasn't long until I finished my stretch of required ward duty at Portsmouth and I was ready for my first real duty station. It was in the summer of 1966 that I got my orders to the Subic Bay Naval Hospital in the Philippines. I was pretty excited about this move. Some of the patients that I talked with had been there and they told me it was a beautiful place. I discovered they were right.

As it turned out I ended up spending just one year at Subic and I was able to complete my High School Education during my stay. I worked on the medical/surgical ward at first and then I was transferred to the orthopedic ward. I liked it better. On my duty nights I was assigned to the emergency room. We saw a great variety of emergencies there and I gained some needed experience that I would draw upon in months ahead. I was introduced to the concept of triage or how to categorize the seriousness of injuries at Subic. I learned to suture. I learned how to prepare doses of various medications and start intravenous fluids. I observed many of the techniques and procedures that were used on both the medical/surgical and orthopedic wards. I was introduced to some of the basic principles of psychiatric medicine.

Many of our patients at the hospital were wounded Marines who had been injured in Vietnam. We treated them with upmost respect and did everything we could to provide care and comfort to them. Most of them were not with us long but were transferred to the U.S. after they were stabilized.

I was called upon one day to accompany a patient from Subic to the larger Air Force Hospital near Angeles City, Philippines. My patient had suffered a ruptured cranial embolism and had to be medevaced immediately. We secured him in a portable military stretcher and I was to chart his blood pressure every fifteen minutes en route to the hospital. We carefully placed our patient in one of the hospital's ambulances and the driver sped us away as I began my duties as the attendant. I observed him cautiously as we drove along. When we arrived at the airstrip we moved him from the ambulance to the small aircraft that would take us on. It was a small plane that was fitted with around a dozen canvas passenger seats and most of them were occupied. We placed my patient in the stretcher in the narrow aisle between the seats and I knelt down and began to care for him. He was unconscious all the way during the flight. I took his blood pressure every fifteen minutes as I was instructed and charted it each time. The flight was quick and soon we began to descend. I wasn't anchored in any way and I began to slide down the aisle somewhat. A big Navy Chief grabbed the back of my belt and secured me. I turned to nod a thank you and he returned my glance. We landed safely. I got help and then we transferred my patient to the hospital. This was my first experience having to medevac anyone but it was a good lesson learned.

After a few months I was promoted to HN (Hospitalman/E3) and transferred to the Orthopedic Clinic. Here I gained greater experience in suturing, bandaging and applying and removing casts and how to set up traction on the ward. I also managed the appointments at the Orthopedic Clinic while assisting two Navy Doctors. Drs. Jensen and Berliner were great men to work for and Dr. Berliner and his beautiful wife gave me a going away party and a Seiko watch with a black face after I received my orders to the Fleet Marine Force. Dr. Berliner said the black face might come in handy where I was going. He also told me to stay down when I heard someone shout incoming!

John and Dr. Bill Berliner, Orthopedic Surgeon (Subic Bay Naval Hospital, Philippines, 1966

I received my orders to the Fifth Marines around August of 1967. I was really surprised but it didn't catch me off guard. By now I had learned that some corpsman served with the Marine Corps. I knew I would be willing and honored to follow in the footsteps of the honorable men who had preceded me. One who comes to mind is John Bradley who was a Fleet Marine Force corpsman in WWII and one of the men who raised the flag at Iwo Jima.

I got another promotion to E4, 3rd Class Petty Officer, toward the end of my tour of duty at Subic and the Navy gave me 20 days leave when I got my new orders. It would be another year before I would be able to take leave again. Twenty days is not much time out of two years. This could have been the last time I would see my family and the last time they would see me. But as they always told us, "due to the needs of the service". The plane ride home was much quicker than the trip over.

Altogether it was a joy to see them again. I didn't think of the short time we would be together. I just took one day at a time and cherished it. I enjoyed my Mother's cooking and my Dad's stories. Our home was a warm, inviting place. We laughed, we played, we enjoyed just being together and we tried to get the most out of my short visit before I had to leave again. I was able to see my church family once more and renew old acquaintances with some of my dear friends.

This is a picture of my brother, Robert, and me in 1967 at the airport in Cincinnati. Here I am wearing my Navy dress blues. I'll be trading them for some Marine Corps green

At home my time flew by so quickly and it wasn't long until my day of departure arrived. My Dad, Mother and family drove me to the Greater Cincinnati Airport. Then we said our farewells and soon I was in the air one more time. As the plane soared along I began to reminisce of my Naval Career thus far. I thought of leaving home for basic training. I remembered trying out for the Drum and Bugle Corps. I thought of my first day at Portsmouth and how so alone I felt. I thought of the memories and friends I had left behind at Subic. I remembered the skill and dedication of the staff that included the doctors, nurses and corpsman. My mind went back to my short visit with my family that had just concluded as I looked out of the airplane window. I didn't know when I would see them again. I didn't know what lay ahead of me. I said a short prayer and asked God for help, protection and guidance.

Isaiah 58:11 *The LORD will guide you continually...* (KJV)

I was to report to Field Medical Training School which was at Marine Corps Base, Camp Pendleton, California. I saw my first "cattle car" there (a modified truck and trailer used as base transportation). It was how you got around on base. It was an experience I have never forgotten. I had not served on a ship. I didn't know much about the sea or ships. I wore a Navy uniform. Up to this point in my military career I had been taught by doctors, nurses and senior corpsman. I had only worked in Naval Hospitals. Now I was entering another phase of my training. I would be trained by Marines. I looked forward to the challenge. I didn't like working inside all of the time. I liked the outdoors. I wanted to be outside. I didn't like the "sterile" atmosphere of the hospital. I wanted to be with the men in green.

I had a dream during my stay in the Philippines. I had dreamed I was on the battlefield. I was kneeling in front of a bush. I was holding and comforting a wounded Marine. The battle was raging all around us but my attention was upon him. I never told anyone about this dream. I just kept it to myself. That dream was fulfilled many times over in the swampy and mountainous regions of Vietnam.

I don't remember all of my preparation at Camp Pendleton but I recall some of it. If you've heard of "shock therapy" then you will know how most of the corpsman felt as we entered our Marine Corps military phase of our training. We had some introduction to the M14. Our weapons training was limited and we did not experience the intense battlefield training the Marines underwent but we had to be familiar with some of the weapons they used and had to quickly adapt to Marine thinking as best we could in such a short time. We were needed on a battlefield far away and we must do our best to be ready.

We had pages and pages of notes from the classrooms and I felt we didn't have enough of "hands on" weapons experience. I wish we could have fired every weapon used by the grunts. However we did throw a few grenades and dig a few "fighting holes" and "hump" a few hills. They did take us through a mock up Vietnamese Village. I remember the lights of Oceanside looked pretty good viewing them at night from the hilltops of Camp Pendleton.

One of our instructors was a salty Marine Corps Sergeant who had healed up from the shrapnel wounds he had gotten in Vietnam. He said once at one of our formations, "I've got enough metal in me to drive a Geiger counter crazy!" He taught us from experience. He was professional and you could feel he had deep respect for corpsman. We felt the seriousness of his instruction and we took it to heart. This Marine had encountered the enemy first hand and had been seriously wounded. He had been administered first aid on the field of battle by a Navy corpsman like myself and was here to bear witness of the importance of our job. A Marine's life may depend on me. I prayed I'd be able to do all I could to the best of my ability. Such a responsibility!

During one of our sessions our instructors tried to relay the seriousness of what lay ahead of us. I can't remember much of the details but one part of the lesson has stayed with me all these years. We were on the grinder standing in formation as our Sergeant addressed us. He was facing our column as we were facing him. There was a group of buildings across the street from us and behind the Sergeant. As he spoke he paused and said, "You men see those buildings behind me?" Well, the one on the end is where they keep the records of all of the MIAs and the KIAs. It is a fact that some of your names will be added to their lists. This was a grim reality that hit home with us. We were dismissed shortly thereafter and most of us walked away without saying much to anyone.

At the mock Vietnamese village set up here we were introduced to the Vietnamese lifestyle. I felt we were rushed through much of our field training but we did learn to march in staggered columns and that chow was to be treated with more respect in the field. We were given examples of hostile situations in which a corpsman might find himself in on the battlefield. The Fleet Marine Force had a plan for everything. We were neither the first nor the last that would be coming through here. We would learn and we would contribute.

I began to realize everything was different now. I had left the sanitary atmosphere of service in a Naval Hospital to find myself in the nitty gritty care of the wounded on the battlefield. I was proud but also apprehensive. I wondered how I would react when someone was shooting at me while I was trying to save the life of a fallen Marine. I hoped and prayed I'd be up to the task.

I was very proud when they issued me a Marine Corps uniform and sea bag. While trying on the "covers" (hats) I thought mine was a little small. The Sergeant looked at me and said, "That fits, Doc. You're going to get a haircut anyway." I've heard it said that once you wear the green you can't go back. That's how most of us felt and I still do. The Marines are a proud brotherhood. "Once a Marine, always a Marine". It has been over 50 years and when I go to the 1st Marine Division Reunions my brothers still call me "Doc". Thank you, brothers.

It seemed like Field Medical Service School was over pretty quickly. I had gotten through some pretty challenging training. I thought I was a pretty efficient corpsman when I entered the School but now I felt more confident. It must have been the Eagle, Globe and Anchor I was now wearing on the collar of my Marine Corps Greens with my Navy rank on my sleeve!

I didn't get any leave after graduating. I had 20 days after my year in the Philippines and now I was headed for another year of duty before I'd be able to take any more providing I survived! I tried to maintain a positive attitude and I relied on my faith in a personal God who was bigger than me. Some of our medical training was that we learned how to control our emotions when treating an injured person. Now I had to psych myself out and keep placing one foot in front of the other and continue down the path life had laid out in front of me. I had to place my trust in God.

Psalms 20:7 *Some trust in chariots and some in horses, but we trust in the name of the LORD our God.* (KJV)

As I recall my group flew out of Travis Air Force Base to Okinawa. This was a stopover for all Fleet Marine Force personnel before going on to Vietnam. We had our sea bags checked and they made sure our shots were up to date and our records were all in order. We were told we would be getting bush uniforms when we got to 'Nam. I had one pair of starched utilities in my sea bag. I was intent on saving them for the day my tour of duty was over and I would wear them on my departure flight home from Vietnam.

Chapter 3

Battle Prepped

(091800H (On September 9, 1967 at 8 a.m.) Company C, 1st Battalion, 5th Marines, observed one VC in vicinity (BT 129298) wearing green utilities and carrying pack. Enemy was taken under fire with 70 rounds small arms fire, 7 M-79 rounds with negative results. In his hasty departure he dropped his pack which was recovered by the patrol. Results: 1 BA 286 riggers for electrical blasting caps, one friction type blasting cap; Anti-American propaganda sheets and a record book. All gear forwarded to Regimental S-2 except blasting caps which were destroyed in place. (This information taken from 1/5 Command Chronology)

I believe it was on September 9, 1967 after our brief stopover in Okinawa I boarded another plane along with the men in my group and this time we were headed to Vietnam. All of us were dressed in our clean, starched and pressed green utilities. We didn't know what we were in for. The flight didn't seem long compared to some others I had been on. I had flown on long flights. It took me 36 hours when I flew from California to the Philippines in 1966. It was aboard a propeller driven aircraft. I remember the flight well because an Admiral was on board and was very friendly and talkative to us enlisted men. He seemed very interested in us. He asked us a few questions about where we had been stationed and about where we were going. He related some of his experiences with us. That was a long but enjoyable flight. We made several stops to refuel on the way over. I remember our plane having to land on Wake Island which was a fierce battlefield in World War 2. It looked like a horseshoe from the windows of our plane. The pilot circled the island a bit and then we made the landing easily, refueled and were quickly on our way. This was a once in a lifetime experience and many of us were disappointed that we were not allowed to leave the aircraft. We just wanted to place our feet on the island and say we had been there on foot but it wasn't to be.

This time, on this aircraft, we were on our way to war! Our apprehensions of the situations ahead of us were mounting. We would soon be introduced to an environment we could never have imagined. No war movie could ever depict what we were going to see. No story teller could ever make us feel the emotions we would experience. We were going to war! This was reality! It was happening! No one can prevent it! It was now I had to pray and ask God for His divine hand of protection as each moment brought me nearer to war.

I was prepared. I had completed my training successfully. I had willingly accepted my orders. Each person has his own way to prepare for a momentous occurrence in his life such as this. My way was to have a little talk with Jesus. I believe in prayer and I believe God answers prayer. I am a living testimony of this fact. When we face deep adversity, when our emotions overwhelm us, when there seems to be nowhere to run, run to The Lord for there you will be safe.

Proverbs 21:31 *The horse is prepared against the day of battle: but safety is of the LORD.* (KJV)

As the aircraft continued on its way my mind began to wander once again. I thought of my roots in the hills of Kentucky. I remembered running through the fields with my brothers and carrying water from our natural spring in lard buckets back to our waiting Mother. I remembered picking wild berries that we called dewberries with which Mother would make scrumptious jelly to put on homemade biscuits for some "starving" kids.

I reminisced of a day in our youth when my brother, Robert and I were off wandering through the country side and getting a little tired so we made it to the top of one of those Kentucky hills. It was summer and the grass was an almost luminescent green so we just plopped down for a break. As we lay on our backs we looked up at the beautiful blue sky with those wonderful fairytale like clouds floating by. We tried to visualize what each one resembled. Like most kids we had great imaginations. The birds were singing soothing melodies in the trees and often a picturesque butterfly would float gently past us.

Loudermilk

I remembered my school days in Cincinnati, Ohio and my friends at Church that I had left behind when I enlisted in the Navy. I thought of my past year of duty in the Philippines and how I enjoyed the weather, the swimming, and the great food at the hospital. We had a couple of great cooks and whenever I had the night duty shift on my ward they would give me a key to the fridge so I could cook whatever I wanted. I had steak quite often!

I used to walk quite a ways down to the air station at Cubi Point and go swimming about two or three times a week. I was in pretty good shape when I left the Philippines. I weighed about 135 pounds when I arrived in 1966 and 186 pounds when I left a year later.

I was physically healthy, spiritually prepared and mentally alert. At least I thought I was. I had many thoughts about what the future would hold. I knew I would be stationed with the best of the best. I had gained confidence and pride in my training. I felt I was as prepared as I could get but still one doesn't know how he will perform when he is faced with the real deal. Only time would tell.

Vietnam was coming in sight! We began to see land ahead as the pilot circled the aircraft. It looked like some pictures I had seen. All I remember was the thick, green jungle and the heat. Like one of my friends, Harold Thrasher, wrote in his book ("Suicide Charlie, Brothers Never Forgotten"), "When they opened the door of the plane it was like opening an oven door". The air was thick and hard to breathe at first. You began to sweat almost immediately upon exiting. The runway was hot and steamy. There was much activity as we walked toward one of the buildings. Everyone was so busy. They all seemed like they had a very important place to go or something very important to do. I just looked around. I smelled the fumes of the aircraft and heard the roar of the engines. Men were trying to yell over the noise as they worked. I noticed the tree line and the mountains in the distance.

I had so many questions running through my mind. I had come a long ways since I enlisted. I had accumulated many new skills. I had gained much experience in the medical field. I had learned from great teachers but still I wondered how I would do. I wanted to be accepted. I wanted to contribute. I wanted to fit in. I hoped I would be able to handle whatever task may be thrown at me. I was beginning to understand that a great responsibility had been placed on my teenage shoulders. I was no longer that seventeen year old kid. I had changed somewhat. A great task had been placed on my young shoulders and now I had to face it.

As we continued to walk we were directed to an area which would be our temporary home for a few days. The heat was sweltering. We were all sweating profusely. I thought to myself, "I sure hope I can get used to this." I thought the Philippines was hot but somehow this place seemed intense.

I was quickly becoming aware of the reality of my new surroundings. The sights, the sounds, the scenery, the smells, the seriousness of it all; this was Vietnam! I was here. I would be here for a year providing I survive. Soon I'll board a helicopter and be flown deep into the jungles and land on a hill where the men who have gone before me have established. I will join their group and become one of them. I will learn to survive with them and by the Grace of God I'll make it.

Somewhere during that time I wrote my first letter home. I had already learned how wonderful it was to get a letter from home and I figured my folks would like to get a letter from me letting them know that I had arrived to Vietnam safely.

I was placed with a group of corpsman and it was good that we spent a little while together in this strange new land but our time together was short lived and soon we were separated and placed into our designated companies. I was assigned to Charlie Company, First Battalion/Fifth Marines. They were dug in on Hill 51. I had no idea where Hill 51 was. All I was told was that it was somewhere north of Danang and in the jungle from where I was at the present. I had to wait on my ride to the Hill. They said that you couldn't get there by trucks. You had to fly. I can't remember how long it was before I flew out but soon a "Jolly Green Giant" helicopter landed and I was instructed to get my gear and get on board. I was not the only passenger. There were a few other men aboard. There were also a few Vietnamese people who were escorting the remains of their village chief back to his home village for burial. It was an ominous site. It was a good thing I wasn't superstitious because this would not have been good.

This was my first experience of flying in country. This aircraft seemed slow but sure. It was a huge helicopter. The rotors spun in a peculiar and loud whirring fashion as they beat the air loudly while we flew along. Out of curiosity I took a peek out of the opened door to get my first close look at the jungle and rice paddies below us. There was a machine gunner sitting there on the ready in case he was needed skillfully grasping his belt fed M60 machine gun. He looked battle weary as he glanced over the area below us. His uniform seemed like he had worn it for a long time. The green color was somewhat washed away and the salty look of an experienced Marine was evident. He had some rips in his trousers and his shirt sleeves were cuffed up above his elbows. I was used to clean surroundings because I had to be careful in the hospital and clinics where I had been working. I was used to starched uniforms and covers at Camp Pendleton. This was going to be drastically different. I had to learn the ropes and find my place in the group.

We flew along slowly but consistently without anyone saying a word and soon we arrived on Hill 51. It was late afternoon and evening chow had been served. We were a little hungry because we had missed our supper. We soon learned we had not been forgotten because they took us to the mess tent promptly and we had our first meal in the bush. I remember it well. We had "homemade" bread and thick green pea soup. I was hungry and ate mine but I noticed the bread had black specks in it. I just thought it was some kind of sesame seeds or something. I learned later it was some kind of beetle that invaded the flour canisters. The cooks just said it was more protein and we got used to it after a while.

Preparing For the Valleys Ahead

I began to pray The Lord's Prayer, after I was assigned to Charlie Company on Hill 51. I continued to always pray this prayer whenever I left our compound whether I was going on a patrol, an ambush, a mine sweep, a convoy or whatever. This prayer became a genuine comfort to me. I felt God would watch over us if we acknowledged him. This prayer became very important to me.

Psalms 23
The LORD is my shepherd; I shall not want.
He maketh me to lie down in green pastures: he leadeth me beside the still waters.
He restoreth my soul: he leadeth me in the paths of righteousness for his name's sake.
Yea, though I walk through the valley of the shadow of death, I will fear no evil: for thou art with me; thy rod and thy staff they comfort me.
Thou preparest a table before me in the presence of mine enemies: thou anointest my head with oil; my cup runneth over.

Battlefield Faith

Surely goodness and mercy shall follow me all the days of my life: and I will dwell in the house of the LORD for ever. Amen (KJV)

Dear Mother, Dad & Family,

Well, I am here in Viet Nam & I still can't believe it. I got here last night. We stayed at Okinawa for a while before coming here.

I am in a line company but I don't know if I will be in an aid station or go out with the marines yet or not.

The weather here is about the same as the Phillipines.

> Send me some paper & an envelope each time you write so I can write a lot. The mail is free here so I'll write every chance I get. I really need your prayers now, worse than I have ever needed them.
>
> Well, I'll close now, but write soon.
>
> Love,
> John

    I was initiated my first night on Hill 51 when we were awakened by an alarm and men shouting and scurrying about in the night. I was with some other new men in the tent where I slept. This was all fresh to us and we instinctively responded to our training methods. We hurriedly made our way to our bunker and waited without knowing what to expect. We had not been assigned any designated responsibility yet so we just waited in the bunker. We heard explosions and saw fire light up the sky in the distance. All we could do was to wait for someone to tell us what was going on or give us direction on what we were supposed to do. We just waited and waited. We were hoping the all clear would sound soon. We had no idea what was happening outside of our bunker. It could have been anything. After all we were in the middle of Vietnam. We were at war. We were hundreds but we were surrounded by enemy soldiers numbering in the thousands. We had faith in our training, we had confidence in the Corps and we learned to trust God.

> Dear Mother, Dad & Family,
> Well, another day has gone by and I'm closer to getting out. I found out that I'm only suppose to be here for 12 month so if everything goes as it should I'll be home next September. I get my choice of duty stations when I get out of here so I'll probably choose Great Lakes, Ill. so I can drive home every week-end.

> Last night we were awaken again but time our ammunition dump was on fire.
>
> They got us all up & we were ordered to put our helmets & flack jackets on. Then we ran to our bunkers (that's a shelter built out of sandbags.) It seemed pretty quiet so we came outside to look, after having stayed in there for about 5 minutes, but then something exploded & we all hit the deck. Some scrapnel went flying but none of the corpsmen were hurt, although we had a few marines that were fighting the fire come in for aid.
>
> Well, alls quiet for now. I know the Lord is with me because when I went to bed before this happened I felt like something was going to erupt in the night so I was ready.
>
> Pray For Me

There was no slack time in Vietnam. We didn't take breaks because of the rain. It seemed that sometimes we went for days soaking wet. Somewhere there was a Vietcong setting a booby trap. The NVA soldiers from the North were continually infiltrating into the South. The local lifestyles were threatened; innocent farmers and their families were tortured and killed. Communities were overrun and children as well as adults were slain. Communism was harsh. Its methods were cruel. The rights of the individual were quickly taken away for the sake of the invading party. The local people feared the approaching enemy. We were there to help them. We were their protectors. Often they did not understand us but were the good guys!

    I learned another Marine tactic on Hill 51. At dusk on the hill everyone had to put on their battle gear which included their helmets, flak jackets and weapons (corpsman, their Unit One Medical bags) and stand shoulder to shoulder spaced accordingly all around the hill. I imagine everyone else was thinking like I was. I wondered if there was any Vietcong in those bushes just a little ways outside our perimeter. I wondered if they were watching us from a distance like we were looking for them. With the enemy all around I still felt comfortable enough to go back to my tent and lay my head down for some needed rest when the word was given to secure. We took comfort in knowing we had one another's back. There was always someone on watch. We never stood alone. We were brothers in arms. Each of us had come from a different place. We had come from all walks of life but we learned how to live together. We learned to respect one another. We were Americans and we were part of the 1st Marine Division.

Dear Mother, Dad, & Family,

Well, I've been in Viet Nam for a week now and only once were we supposedly under attack. They sounded Red Alert and we went to the shelter and in 10 minutes or so they secured it and we went back to bed. Right now I'm with the 5th marines, 1st battalion, 1st Marine Division. The most decorated battalion in this division. I'm proud to be with them. They are nicknamed "The Fightin' Fifth."

We are sleeping in tents while here at camp but when we go on patrol we sleep on the ground. Luckily, I haven't been on patrol yet.

Oh yes, we're not supposed to carry rifles but are

issued .45 caliber pistols for our own protection and our patients. Right now it is raining & will rain now every day because the monsoons are starting. Actually I'm lucky to have come here this time of the year because everything is black.

Sometimes we got tired just standing there staring into the dusk as the sun slowly sank over the mountains. The lush greenery was replaced by evening shadows. Soon we would be able to stand down. In just a little while darkness fell upon us. Then we were permitted to return to our tents for the night unless we were on duty but just before dawn we had to go back to our posts and stay until daylight. This was to make the enemy think we had stood there all night. We did this each evening. After a while it became a routine. Our safety depended upon it.

Dear Mother, Dad, & Family,

I just received your first letter ~~today~~ dated 27 Sept. It sure is a big morale booster.

You asked me several questions & here the answers:

① Yes, I did get the money you sent it sure did help me out.

② I left my clothes in Okinawa, in ~~storage~~. I just brought my utilities with me, and I got issued 2 more sets of jungle utilities & 1 pair of boots (jungle).

③ I have a rain coat, but the rains here are quite different than back home ~~there~~. They are more fierce.

I am never in one place long enough to say where I am but I have been in the jungle staying in tents most of the time.

Mother, I surely think the Lord is definitely helping me out because we have been moved from a line company back to rear security. I only had to go out in the jungle twice & both times we weren't fired upon so I know God is surely with me. I am supposed to only spend 6 months with this company and then go to the rear anyway so I know if it is God's will, I will be in the rear the rest of my time here.

Well, I'll write again soon so please pray for me.

Love,
John

P.S. write soon

Chapter 4

Earning My Salt

(Command Chronology for period 1-31 October 1967) Enemy activity during the month was restricted mainly to sniping by individuals of small units and placing mines and booby traps throughout the TAOR, especially in the northern area. However, an estimated local force of one to two platoons did probe the perimeter of CAP D-5 on three occasions and contact was made by a platoon of Company B on 28 October with an estimated platoon of Viet Cong in the vicinity of DT 127607. Reports of the Q-15 company in the northern, the Q-12 Company in the eastern and southeastern and a company of the T-05 Battalion in the northwestern portions of the TAOR were received. Although no positive contact with or identification of these units was made, activity and sightings within these areas partially support the presence of such units. Additionally, elements of the 70th Independent Battalion and the V-25 Battalion were reported to be operating in and to the south of the Island complex in the southeastern area of the TAOR. Again, no positive contact or identification was made; but sightings of military structures, fighting positions, and enemy river traffic by airborne observers indicate the presence of enemy units in these areas.

(This information taken from November 1967 Command Chronology, 1st Battalion/5th Marines)

I was surprised to see a Chapel of any sort constructed way out here on this outpost but the Marines had one built out of bamboo and it served the purpose. Someone said it cost $300.00.

Dear Mother, Dad & Family,

Well, another day has gone by & the rains are here. Right now its pouring down rain and the wind is blowing pretty hard. It almost blew a couple of poles over that are holding our tent up.

Life here has not been to bad so far, although I haven't been on patrol yet. I want you all to pray for me because we are going on an operation Saturday. We're going on a company sweep. That's where our company goes throughout the area looking for V.C. and clearing them out.

I went to church Sunday before last & the Chaplain is pretty good. He is a man of God, I believe. We have a chapel which was constructed by the Vietnamese for $300.00, although its made of bamboo.

Battlefield Faith

We Americans had brought our Judeo-Christian faith with us. I wanted to let my family know about the Chapel. When I wrote home I always tried to reassure them that I was well and had somewhat of a structured life regardless of my wartime circumstances. The longer I was in the bush the more hardened I became but I did not realize it at the time. In combat you have to become tough in order to survive. You learn to keep your emotions to yourself. I still believed God had his hand on me but the horrible scenes I would witness had an effect on my human persona. Like everyone else I was once a "new guy" and like them I had to start somewhere.

It was usually customary that the new men were allowed a couple of days to get accustomed to the climate upon their arrival. During this interval we had to attend some mandatory classes about survival in the bush but this time passed quickly and soon we took our places with the other men. It so happened when I arrived in country our regiment was right in the middle of Operation Swift which was a bloody endeavor. I was one of the replacements for a corpsman who had been a casualty of this battle. I remember beginning my routine of going on patrols and ambushes and having to acquaint myself with the squad leaders and the men of the different squads. All of the squad leaders were perfectionists. They each had their own styles of leadership. Each patrol or ambush was different. Each ambush was set up in a different place. One night we would position ourselves in a cemetery and at other times we were near artillery that fired all night long. Sometimes we were near rivers and other times on hilly terrain. We never went to the same place twice. We were always searching for the enemy and hoping to find him before he found us.

Loudermilk

> Sunday
> 15 October 67
>
> Dear Mother, Dad & Family,
>
> Well, I thought I'd write you a few lines to let you know how everything is going.
>
> I went on another mine sweep of the main road this morning at 0630 & went on patrol at 0900. We didn't see anything much.
>
> The Lord is still watching over me. We heard a couple of stray rounds but they were probably allied forces.
>
> Did you ever get those pictures developed that I had taken? Write and tell me if they turned out.
>
> Well, I'll close now but write soon.
>
> Love,
> John

That first patrol was very challenging for me and I know many men have felt the same way. The experience was much like teaching someone to swim by having them jump into deep water and try and swim their way to shore. I was very vigilant and I guess my nerves were showing. The squad leader had assigned a combat hardened Marine to walk behind me in the column and keep a close eye on me so I wouldn't do anything stupid. I veered off

Battlefield Faith

the trail a time or two and he motioned to me so that I knew exactly what he meant without a word being spoken. There would be many patrols and ambushes ahead of me but I remember this first one very well. I learned that each step I took had to be carefully placed. I learned I had to become a contributing member of each squad to which I was assigned. I didn't want to be a liability but an asset.

    Two corpsmen were usually assigned to a platoon. I met the other corpsman upon my arrival to Charlie Company. His name was Jimmy Mathis. He was from New Mexico. I liked him right away. He was soft spoken and seemed like a seasoned veteran to me. He showed me around and tried to bring me up on the latest happenings. We would be taking turns with the ambushes and patrols, mine sweeps and convoys. Wherever you found Marines you would find a corpsman.

Monday
30 October '6)

Dear Mother, Dad & Family,

Well, I thought I drop you a few lines and say everything going fine while I have time. They sure are pushing us these past couple of days. We were in a fight the other night, bullets were flying everywhere and 2 men were hit. My buddie ran to the one in front and bandaged him up while I took care of the other one. My buddie is going to get the Bronze Star for treating that guy in the line of fire. He was really taking a chance. I was behind a high trench treating my patient. I thank God for watching over me. We set up an

Battlefield Faith

> ambush last night but no "Gooks" came around, so we didn't shoot any. Well, I'll close for now and be sure to pray for me.
>
> Love,
> John
>
> P.S. Write soon. I think I'm getting all your letters now.

　　I remember seeing Jimmy in action. Whenever the entire platoon went out both corpsman had to go otherwise we would rotate with the squads on our other assignments. I recall this one particular time we went out on a platoon operation. We patrolled what seemed like many miles and as the day drew on the sun began to fade away. Our platoon leader knew it was time to settle in for the night and set up our perimeter, send out listening posts and assign our ambush positions. We found a suitable site near a rustling river for the platoon. Each of the Marines seemed to intuitively take his fighting position for the night. Jimmy and I took our positions also and this evening we were able to spend some time together before settling in and before we would have to face whatever the night might bring. We sat and talked a little while as we heated our c-ration hot chocolate up with a heat tab. We were enjoying our short visit and were talking about home and other things.

However before the temperature got just right on our cocoa a shot rang out, then another. The enemy was seen and we began to exchange fire. The enemy soldiers were across the river and a ferocious battle had begun. Instinctively we quickly gathered our gear and hurried to the action as we split up. Someone ahead yelled, "Corpsman!" Jimmy took off across the river rocks. I found myself some cover in a ditch near the rocket man to wait for another call for help. No sooner did I get settled when he prepared to fire his weapon. But before firing he turned around to make sure all was clear, as he was trained, and saw me. He said "Doc', you don't want to be there when I fire. That's another "stupid" thing that new guys do. I was paying so much attention to the battle ahead and listening for the call of an injured Marine that I overlooked the Marine with the 3.5 rocket launcher. I instantly moved away and he fired his weapon.

My friend, Marine Mike Short, holding the 3.5

Battlefield Faith

    The tracer rounds were viciously streaking through the air in both directions. Jimmy scrambled haphazardly across the rough terrain determined to make his way to the wounded Marine who had been hit by an enemy round and had fallen on the river rocks still clutching his weapon. I could see the river just a few yards ahead of them. Jimmy bravely tended to the injured man's wounds while kneeling on the unforgiving ground. He appeared to ignore the tracer rounds that whizzed past him as he worked. As the battle raged another Marine called out, "corpsman!" It was now my turn. The tracers seemed to become more intense. I took off from where I was positioned as fast as I could in a running crawl across the rocks. I had so much adrenaline flowing I paid them no attention. I only had that wounded Marine on my mind. The incoming small arms rounds were hitting the rocks and they splattered all around us as each man focused his attention on our adversary across the river. I made it to the wounded man and immediately saw the area of his wounds. His shirt was blood soaked and he appeared to be in severe pain. I began the task of cleaning and treating the ripped flesh and bone the enemy's weapon had produced. I tried my best to comfort him and reassure him we would get him out of here as quickly as possible. The battle raged on for what seemed like hours as hot lead shrieked in both directions and Jimmy and I were kept very busy in our tasks of assisting the Marines who had fallen.
    Soon we gained the edge on our enemies and the firing slacked off. Our Platoon Commander then sent a squad across the river to secure the area and find out what they could about our adversaries. Our radioman then began to call for a medevac for our injured men. We had to create a landing zone by clearing out the area for the arrival of the chopper and when it arrived we carefully placed our wounded men on board. The chopper did not hesitate and as soon as the last man was loaded on board the engine raced loudly as the rotors whirred furiously and the aircraft began to lift off. The smell of the exhaust, the stench of sweat mixed with blood, the trees and bushes being blown in all directions by the chopper and the shouts of the men on the ground is something I will never forget.
    For a few moments from the time the first shot was heard it seemed like organized chaos but the Marines are a finely tuned combat machine and eventually everything gradually settled down and the guys began to talk a little. The enemy had been overwhelmed and had run away deep into the jungle. This time our firepower was too much for them. Someone said the

enemy soldiers had a woman squad leader. All Jimmy and I knew is that when we returned to our little area we would not have any cocoa this night. We had knocked our cups over on our hasty exit. It was a shame we had wasted two good heat tabs. We didn't always have them and we often ate cold chow, grease and all. Ham and lima beans were the most difficult to eat cold but regardless of that I always ate whatever I had because I knew I needed the calories although I didn't get many. I remember Jimmy always gave me his apricots. I never turned down any food.

Up to this point I hadn't noticed my trouser legs but it did seem a little drafty going back to the hill the next morning. Our Lieutenant (who was from Cincinnati, Ohio and had taught at Oak Hills High School where some of my friends had attended) came over to me and said, "Doc, you need to go over to supply and get yourself another pair of trousers." It was then that I looked down and my trouser knees were completely out on both legs and my legs were scratched, blackened and a little bloody from the river rocks. I walked into supply and the supply Sergeant took one look at me and said, "Doc, What happened to you?" I replied, "It's a long story." With a puzzled look in his eye he had someone get me a new pair of trousers. I learned as I gained more experience that you see many things in the bush that you didn't in training.

We resumed our routine back on Hill 51. As far as I know we didn't have a barber on the hill and I was a little reluctant when I was told I had to go into town to get a haircut. It wasn't much of a town. It was more like a village that had sprung up because of our presence in the area. Since we didn't have our own barber there was no choice. We didn't go anywhere alone so a friend went with me and I guess he may have gotten a haircut too. He knew where to go so I followed his lead and we found a shack that had been put up and a local older man was waiting for a customer. As I sat in his chair he didn't speak a word. He didn't know any English and I didn't know any Vietnamese so there wasn't any conversation going on. It was much different than most of the barber shops I had been accustomed to. When he was finished I paid him and when I looked in his small mirror I thought he actually did a pretty good job. The only problem was since my hair was already short I told him to just take a little off as I motioned with my fingers but instead he left just a little on! When I paid him he most graciously accepted the money which was MPC (Military Payment Certificate) with many bows and a wide smile that showed what looked like gold fillings in his teeth.

My friend and I thought we would check out the other shops and we just walked around a bit noticing the various items the villagers had for sale. We may have gotten us something to eat and in a little while the evening shadows began to gather so we figured we had better get back to the hill.

The next morning it was my turn to go on patrol. Our squad assembled in the company area before we moved out. Each man made sure he had all the gear that he needed. We looked one another over and then we walked out of the gate. We walked for quite a distance until we stopped at one of the many hooches that dotted the countryside. A Mama San greeted us openly and offered us some ripe bananas to eat. Once again I noted that wide smile and oriental bowing. Most of the villagers were very courteous to us. I don't know if this was because they feared us or were grateful we had come to drive the invaders out. In any event most of them were respectful and we were cautious.

As we continued our patrol we came across a boy that had suffered an injury and still had a small issue of blood. The squad leader called "corpsman Up" and I made my way to where the boy was sitting on the ground. I examined him quickly and I detected it was only superficial so I cleaned his wound as best I could then bandaged him up. Many times these kids were the victims of booby traps set by our enemy. They were placed over trails that the villagers frequented daily in hopes that we might come along and trip them but unfortunately it was often their own that they killed or injured.

After our stop we continued on. We walked and walked and soon our squad leader said, "Take five." We were ready for a break. We all spread out and found a place to relax for a few minutes. Many times we would carry an extra pair of socks on our packs to air out and we would change sometime during our patrol. It seemed like we were always getting our feet wet. We took turns as we did this and always kept an eye out for the enemy. This time we hadn't stopped for long when we heard some rustling of the vegetation down the path behind us. Each man made ready but in a moment we heard the voices of some kids. They were yelling, "Coca, Coca!" In a moment to our surprise in walked some youngsters carrying what looked like makeshift coolers and to our astonishment they had Coca Colas for sale and they were cool. They were asking $5.00 per small bottle of Coke. We never could figure out how they could be following us without making any detectable noise but more than this, "How did they keep those Cokes cool when the temperature had to be close to 100 degrees or more!

I remember thinking as I was becoming more accustomed to my surroundings that God had made us all. These kids who brought us the cokes were not all that much different than we were at that age but many of them had their minds poisoned by communist propaganda. However, they were cheerful little guys and I kind of felt sorry for them being caught in the middle of a war. And I remember some scripture that fits this scene.

Acts 17:24-26 *God that made the world and all things therein, seeing that he is Lord of heaven and earth, dwelleth not in temples made with hands;*
Neither is worshipped with men's hands, as though he needed any thing, seeing he giveth to all life, and breath, and all things;

Battlefield Faith

And hath made of one blood all nations of men for to dwell on all the face of the earth, and hath determined the times before appointed, and the bounds of their habitation; (KJV)

We have all been created in the image of GOD. Growing up we were taught to "do unto others as you would have them do unto you" and most people lived by that ideal where I was from. But here it was a different story. There was a gulf between us and the people we had come here to help.

The people were different than any I had ever met or seen in my life. They were tough. At first glance they appeared to be physically weak but I came to realize they were inwardly strong. They had become accustomed to the lifestyle they were living from childhood. Most of them had no luxuries. Most had meager necessities. I became more acquainted with the farmers and villagers and fishermen during my year of duty than with the city dwellers with only a short while spent in Hue City. These Vietnamese people just didn't live in any way I had ever experienced. They looked different. Their clothes were strange looking which mostly consisted of pajama like shirt and trousers and a cone shaped straw hat. Sandals adorned their feet and most of the older people I saw were flat footed. Often the adults had blackened teeth from chewing "beetlenut". I think the nut had some kind of narcotic effect when chewed. We followed a trail once that we thought was blood. After a while we saw a Vietnamese ahead and yelled for them to stop. We were surprised when we realized we had been following a person that was chewing beetlenut and spitting much like Americans do who chew tobacco.

The enemy, Vietcong, dressed in what we called, "black pajamas". He wore the cone shaped straw hat too. We captured a few of them in the year I was in country. Just about all of them seemed to be flat footed. I remember one particular Vietcong we captured who had enormous flat feet. He was adorned in his "black pajamas". He kept smiling at us but we could see through his deceitful eyes. He was caught in the act of firing at us. Many of the villagers were afraid of guys like him. He spoke their language. He knew how to adapt and appear as a local when in reality he may have been part of an invading army that had walked through the jungles all the way from Hanoi to infiltrate into the local population. This particular Vietcong had some battle scars. His face was weather weary. Overall he looked pretty healthy. Evidently he had been getting enough to eat. Guys like him robbed the locals and took food from them. Often it was food that was sent as care packages from the United States to feed hungry local populations.

The villagers lived in straw huts we called "hooches". If they had a bed it was made of bamboo wood. The looks on their faces appeared to say I don't trust you but I will tolerate you for a while because just as the soldiers before you I know you won't be here long. We were passing through a village once while on one of our many patrols. We stopped for a break from the heat and rest a while. I saw an old man squatting over a homemade fire with a small kettle over it. He motioned for me to come over and I did. He motioned again and this time for me to take a cup. I did and then he reached over to the blackened pot hanging above the fire on the ground and began to pour and fill my cup with a liquid he had in it. I saw him drink from another cup after he had poured some for himself so I felt it was safe. It looked like very weak tea and it was. I took a sip, looked at him as he looked at me with a smile on his weary weather beaten face. I said thank you in my best high school French and we enjoyed the tea together. He spoke a few words in French and I tried my best to reply. We had a good visit and I shall remember that aged Asian gentleman for a long time. I thought to myself maybe they're not all bad. No matter how nice they were or how well they seemed to act you couldn't trust any of the locals. One of the biggest gaps in our endeavors was our communication or lack thereof. Most of us were not taught any of the local languages during our hurried training at Camp Pendleton.

The Vietcong knew how the Americans felt about kids and senior people so they used that against us. I recall hearing about a jeep driver who gave an elderly woman a ride. When he stopped to let her off he didn't see the bag she ominously left behind. She smiled and waved goodbye as he drove off. A few yards down the road the bag which held an explosive device blasted and the Marine was killed and the jeep destroyed as the old Viet Cong woman walked away.

Our patrols went out every day regardless of the weather. We walked over all kinds of terrain ranging from swamps to mountain peaks. The swamps and rice paddies were tough going sometimes. We sloshed our way through the mud of the rice paddies which was often up to our knees only stopping to get the leeches off when we reached dry land.

> Dear Mother, Dad & family,
>
> Well, thought I'd write you all a few lines to let you know everything is going just fine and I'm in real good health and the Lord is helping me every day.
>
> Sandy sent me an anointed cloth (handkerchief) and I now have that to carry.
>
> It's pretty cool here now and rains a little bit every day. Why don't you send me 2 rain suits instead of one. They wear out pretty quick here with all the thorns and barb wire.
>
> We were down at the ocean the other night looking for "gooks" and just got back today from being out for 2 days.

    We got into firefights in these places very often. You either had to get down in the mud or try and make it to the other side. If a man went down I had to go to him and try to get the both of us to safety or wait for help as the firing continued. Often it wasn't very pretty. We never left any man. We always did our best to save those we could and rescue the Marines who needed our help. All of the Marines were brave men. I only knew heroes. In the States during my tour of duty they were having some racial problems but on the battlefield there wasn't any black and white. There was only green! We were young men. Some in the States considered us boys but we were men with a man's responsibility. We carried the power of life and death in our hands. We had the authority of our government and the blessing of the South Vietnamese government to expel the northern aggressors and their collaborators from this land. We had to be wise. Our very lives depended on it. We had to discern between friend and foe and that was a very perplexing task.

Matthew 10:16 ... *be ye therefore wise as serpents, and harmless as doves.* (KJV)

Many times when we would go through a small village there would be no one there. Once while participating in a search and destroy mission we passed through an area that was classified as enemy territory. When we passed through the village an old woman was the only person we saw. We couldn't help but notice her looking at us and our gear pretty inquisitively. The men and squad leader figured out that she was taking notes for the Vietcong for when they returned. We didn't harm her but while she argued or cussed us in her language the Marines tied her up so she wouldn't be able to quickly run to them and tell them of our number and position as soon as we were out of sight. We didn't want them coming in the "back door" and hitting us from the rear. We couldn't give them that advantage.

There was another story of a Marine squad that was passing through a village similar to this one and a kid walked over to them and reached out his hand. When he did a grenade exploded killing him and a few of the Marines near the blast. The Marines may have had chocolate to give him but the enemy had poisoned his young mind and he was killed. You couldn't let down your guard for an instant. Like the men with whom I shared food and water and life itself, like them I became as an animal in the wild. I was always watching for something unusual. I listened for anything that I thought was out of the ordinary. Ones senses become heightened in war. Look at the squirrel. He is constantly on the move. His eyes and ears sense danger. An unknown noise sends him running. The deer walk slowly. They look. They listen. They smell. If anything is different or unrecognizable they turn and run. They don't hang around to ask questions. Their life depends on it. You have to think, "How quiet would it be if I wasn't standing here or walking here?" You have to look for peculiarities and unusual things. You must learn not to be careless.

    I didn't really comprehend the extent of my duty here. Jim and I and all of the Grunt (infantry) corpsman had to go out on every ambush, every patrol, mine sweeps, convoy duty, etc. We had an awesome responsibility. We took one day and one night at a time. Each morning brought you closer to the day of your rotation home. I continued to write home and reassure my family that I was doing ok.

Dear Mother, Dad, & Family,

Well, I'm writing to let you know everything is going just fine & alright etc.

We got out of the bush country a couple a days ago & have been guarding a bridge since. We are in a bunker & haven't had any trouble yet.

We now have a mascot; it's a little pup. We call him Ralph. He's a pretty cute little dog. He sleeps right above my head. He's brown with a couple of black spots on his tail.

Oh yes, the bridge we are guarding got blowed up by the V.C. So the Marines built a pontoon bridge & we are guarding both now.

Well, I'll close now but write soon.

Love,
John

P.S. Pray for me.

Chapter 5

No Steak and Eggs

Enemy activity during the month was restricted mainly to sniping by individuals of small units and placing mines and booby traps throughout the TAOR, especially in the northern area. However, an estimated local force of one to two platoons did probe the perimeter of CAP D-5 on three occasions and contact was made by a platoon of Company B on 28 October with an estimated platoon of Viet Cong in the vicinity of DT 127607. Reports of the Q-15 company in the northern, the Q-12 Company in the eastern and southeastern and a company of the T-05 Battalion in the northwestern portions of the TAOR were received. Although no positive contact with or identification of these units was made, activity and sightings within these areas partially support the presence of such units. Additionally, elements of the 70th Independent Battalion and the V-25 Battalion were reported to be operating in and to the south of the Island complex in the southeastern area of the TAOR. Again, no positive contact or identification was made; but sightings of military structures, fighting positions, and enemy river traffic by airborne observers indicate the presence of enemy units in these areas.

(This information taken from Command Chronology, 1st Battalion/5th Marines, October 1967)

I remember an instructor telling us new guys early on at one of our introductory class sessions that the Marines had moved here to the Que Son Valley so that "Charlie" couldn't walk through with his head held high. I learned that my battalion had seen some rough combat in May of this year. I had arrived when my battalion was in the middle of

Operation Swift and these operations were continuing. I remember thinking how incredibly dedicated to the task the officers and enlisted men were. I was deeply impressed at the seriousness of how even the lowest private did his job. I am thankful for all of the men that helped me to adapt to the ways of the Marines. They taught me how to walk the trails while on patrol. I learned to watch as they did for anything out of the ordinary.

I learned how to be quiet while on ambush. I remember while on one of my first ambushes I was so thirsty. We had walked a long ways to our ambush site and had to climb a sharp incline to get to our position for the night. The weather was hot and muggy as usual and once again the sweat on our uniform shirts had turned to a salty white as they began to dry. After we settled in I grabbed my canteen and without thinking began to guzzle the refreshing although warm water. One of the Marines nudged my shoulder and said, "Doc, go easy on that water." I said, "Oh, man, I forgot for an instant. I was so thirsty." The heat and the humidity were extreme. Often we would walk for a long ways before we would stop for a break. I guess since we had taken a long hike to get to this place that I got really thirsty. After that I always remembered. I tried to carry an extra canteen when I went out because I had to be ready in case one of the men suffered a perforated abdominal wound that would require a wet dressing or if I had an injured Marine that was out of water and needed a drink.

The longer I was there the more I learned. Each new day and night brought with it new experiences. It wasn't long before I was an "old salt". I began to learn what items to carry in my Unit One Medical Bag. I carried Morphine in my bag for the seriously wounded. I carried ointments and battle dressings. I was fearful of not having enough bandages so once I asked the Marines to carry at least one battle dressing in a certain pocket so I would know where to look in case I needed it. I also carried a surgical kit and a few other things.

Each of our assignments carried with it a routine every one of us had to establish according to our responsibility to the unit. Each task was dependent and important to the other. We had a point man who was the first man in the column as we walked in staggered columns down the road or single file along the trails in the jungle. A couple of riflemen walked behind him. We had a squad leader who was the Marine in command. We had a radioman that walked in front of me, the corpsman, and behind the squad leader. A rifleman walked behind me and was often my bodyguard when things got hot and heavy. A couple of riflemen walked behind him. We often had a 3 man machine gun team and a rocket man who carried a law, which was a disposable rocket launcher. We always had a rifleman as our rear security. We usually had between 10 to 15 men I would guess on our patrols and ambushes.

We not only had to worry about our enemies weapons. We had other things to content with. The mosquitos were horrendous. We had insect repellant to use when we had it. One of our radiomen hated the bugs so much he had someone from home send him a large can of Raid. I recall him spraying himself one night before we went out on ambush. The squad leader got after him and said the VC were liable to smell him he had used so much. I don't remember him using the Raid after that.

Whenever we walked through the rice paddies, and that was often, we would get leeches on us. We used liquid insect repellant on them if we had it. One squirt on them and they fell off. Some guys would light a cigarette and touch them and they would fall off that way also. I had to medevac an ARVN soldier once who had gotten a leech in his ear so far I couldn't get it out. We helped him get a ride to Danang.

You never knew what would happen next in combat so you had to try your best to be ready. Each new day or night brought a diverse learning experience. You learned how to tie your boots and tie your trouser legs. You adapted to the small amount of food you were allotted on a daily basis. On a good day we got two c-ration meals. Now and then we would get a hot meal. Sometimes we would find food in the various villages we passed through. Once while on a squad patrol we were hungry as usual and we smelled food as we searched the deserted "hooches" of a village in our path. Sometimes the villagers would run and hide when they saw us coming. Occasionally we didn't see them and at other times a Mama San would stay behind to check us out.

As we moved through the area we came upon this particular hooch and it was our routine to carefully look inside. We saw a small table which was set with plates and freshly prepared food upon them. The thing I remember most was the warm greens that hadn't been off of the fire for long. We were hesitant at first and I remembered a story a man had told me when I was in the Philippines that happened in World War 2. The people were used to the Japanese soldiers coming through their villages similarly to what we were doing. But they were destructive. The people feared them. My friend said they poisoned some hot food once and left it on a table knowing the enemy would find it.

We had a difficult decision to make. A man's mentality changes in combat. One Marine told me once that if he was going to be killed he wished it would happen before he "humped" the hills all over Vietnam. We had to determine if it was worth the risk of eating the food or leaving it and continue on our way hungry. We talked a bit. I take no credit but I said a short, silent prayer and I believe some of the other men prayed too. I believe God heard our prayers because none of us got sick and that food was very good. It wasn't something we drank but rather what we ate which we attributed to our prayer. We never let our guard down while we ate.

Mark 16:18 … *and if they drink any deadly thing, it shall not hurt them…* (KJV)

Another time we were on a Platoon size operation which consisted of about fifty men or more. As usual we were hungry. We carefully swept across a field of elephant grass until we came to another village. There were a few villagers there and the Marines checked them out. Then as we moved on through the village we noticed one of the Vietnamese had placed some not yet completely ripe bananas on a flat lid which was sitting on a table to ripen. As we passed by each man took one. I got mine quickly like the rest. As we continued on our walk a few paces I turned to look back and I saw all of the bananas were gone but there were a few happy Marines that had a great unexpected treat this afternoon. We figured it was a small price for the villagers to pay for our protection and we were grateful but we were on the move so we couldn't stop to say thanks this time.

I was out with another squad size patrol at another time. We were walking up the side of this mountain on one of the trails. We had walked a great distance from our outpost so the squad leader had us to stop and take a break. We didn't have much to eat that day either. We noticed a young Vietnamese boy starting to come up the hill and he was prodding a young cow in front of him. The guys began talking. "Some steak would be real good right now", one of the men said. Somebody asked, "Has anyone ever butchered a cow?" One Marine was from the southwest and said, "I have." A couple of other Marines said they would help. The boy was getting closer and had a look of anticipation and bewilderment on his face as he neared our position. The squad leader came over to where we were talking and said, "We're not butchering a cow today." I believe they would have done it. I guess I would have helped if they had asked me. I was hungry just like them.

 We were walking through the bush once. We had been out most of the day when we came to an opening where I noticed a small garden with a few ripened tomatoes. As we drew nearer I said, "I'm going to get me one of those tomatoes when we take five". One of the guys from one of the big cities replied, "Where are we going to get a tomato way out here?" We took our break and ate a few of the ripened tomatoes then another Marine from Louisiana noticed a cane field and said, "How about some desert?" We didn't know what he was talking about at first then he returned with some sugar cane for us to chew on. I had never eaten sugar cane before and this was great.

 I was on another patrol with a different squad some time later. Again we were hungry as usual. When I got home I remember someone asked me about the food we ate and how much we got. I told them I think I had figured it out. I said in combat I believe the Marines keep you a little hungry like I once heard an old hunter say about his dogs, "If they're a little hungry they hunt better". I don't agree with it and I don't think many hunters do but anyways that's the only reasoning I could muster up. I didn't want to think they didn't feed us on purpose.

 But back to the story: When it came time for us to take a break we were again near a village or at least a few hooches. We only saw a few Vietnamese. Some chickens began to meander our way and the Marines began to get that hungry look in their eyes. One Marine walked over to where I was sitting and said, "Doc, would you mind if I borrowed your 45?" I replied, "No, anytime." Sometimes one of our "tunnel rats" would borrow my 45 when they checked out a hole which we would occasionally find where the VC would hide and store their weapons. He said, "We haven't found a tunnel but we wanted to shoot one of these chickens and cook it and I didn't want to use my M16 on it." I said, "Fine with me." We began to get quiet as the chickens slowly moved our way. A young boy about 11 or so started walking over toward us. I think he realized what was about to happen. He said if we would pay for the chicken he would kill it and cook it for us. We pooled our resources and came up with five dollars' worth of MPC. (Military Payment Certificate) We didn't use real currency. The boy said that was fine. By this time we were looking forward to a fried chicken meal. We couldn't wait.

After a while the boy came back with our "fried chicken". Well, it wasn't fried! It was boiled I think and not even hot. Anyways, we each took a piece. The chicken leg I got was like rubber. It had no flavor and didn't even resemble anything that tasted like chicken. Most of us threw it away after trying to take a bite. I guess this was another lesson learned in the bush.

Dear Mother, Dad, & Family,

Just a few lines to let you know whats going on.

Not much has really happend in the past couple of days. I've been on mine-sweeps every morning and go on patrol every other day, rotating with the other corpsman in the platoon, Jim Mathis. He's a pretty good guy.

Its been pretty cool here recently also. I caught a cold and just now getting over it. I never had it to bad. I get plenty of rest here. I hope that it's Gods Will for us to stay here. This is pretty good duty. Pray about it for me.

Well, continue to pray for me and write soon.

Love,
John

Same Place

Battlefield Faith

Like the other guys I was comparing this bit of food to my Mother's fried chicken. I remember the wonderful aroma coming from her kitchen after I would come in from playing outside when I was a kid. When my siblings and I were outdoors in the summertime we didn't come in until we were famished. Often Mother hadn't finished supper yet and I'd be so hungry. If she was preparing coleslaw she would ask if I wanted to chew on the cabbage stalk until everything was ready and my Dad would be home from work. I'd gladly take it and could hardly wait until I could get a piece of that fried chicken. Other times she would tell me to get myself a glass of milk.

I remember whenever Mother fried chicken for the family she always said the back was her favorite part. I didn't know when I was a kid but I think she said that so her family could get the best parts with the most meat. Dad was a hardworking man and hungry when he came home from work in the evening. We would ask him what his favorite part was and he would reply "the breast and all the rest."

We didn't have much to eat in Nam. We were happy with what we did get. We felt like it was a morsel here and there. I learned to appreciate my country and the memories I had of my youth and I was eager to return to it and to my loving family. I suppose some of us get spoiled especially those who have never been out of the country.

I was always concerned my family would worry about my safety. I tried not to alarm them with my writing. I wanted them to know some of what I was experiencing but I didn't want to unjustly cause them unnecessary distress. I was glad when another day would pass. I was thankful for seeing the dawning of a new day. I knew each day would bring me closer to the time I would leave this inauspicious country behind me. I felt happiness would be Vietnam "in my rear view mirror!" We were often told that when we left we would get one of our three choices of duty station. I remember making my choices. It never works out though. It seemed I never got anyplace I ever asked for. I was always assigned according to the needs of the service. You can get it in writing but if the military needs you somewhere else that's where you are going.

The Marines tour of duty was 13 months. A corpsman had to spend 12 months in country. We had to spend 6 months in the field before we were eligible for a reassignment. I remember while I was with the "grunts" (Marine Corps Infantry) I never got really sick. I might have had a cold but nothing serious. I never got a severe wound however I was traumatized by several concussions. I didn't get a rash. I did get a lot of mosquito bites and I don't advise anyone to do what I did. I would make the bite area bleed to get all the poison out and I would dress it with antiseptic salve if I had it. Our battalion surgeon took his malaria tablets judiciously but he still got malaria. He was so frustrated. Thank God I didn't. I was at First Medical Battalion once in Danang for a medevac and I saw them treating a Marine who had Malaria. He was lying on a stretcher and they were giving him an ice water bath. I really felt sorry for him as he lay there shivering but that was the way they got his extremely high fever down.

I was fairly new. I had seen some combat. I had a few experiences but I was still learning. I continued to learn for the rest of my time in 'Nam. I don't think anyone ever gets use to it. You just have to learn to survive as best you can. You have to "go with the flow". You have to be very careful and not get careless. I tried to always ask for my family to pray for me.

My first platoon commander rotated home. I can't recall the reason. I never got to say good bye. I never saw him again after our first few encounters.

I was raised to believe in God. I was taught to trust in God and that He would hear me when I prayed. My parents were sincere Christians. My dad was born in 1906. He had lived through the Great Depression. I asked him a few questions once about his experiences during that time. He said, "We always had plenty to eat in the country. When we would kill a hog we would share with our neighbors. Everybody did that. We would help each other. That was the Christian thing to do." This is the man that raised me and taught me how to treat others. Dad did tell me once, "If you got to fight, fight fair!" Much has changed in our society since his childhood in the '20s.

My Mother was brought up in church. She taught me I should treat others the way I would want to be treated. She told me to play fair. My parents grew up in a rural community where most families knew one another. Most of them had grown up together. Many of them were related to each other in some way.

I continued to visit the Chapel on Hill 51 whenever I could and I had met one of the Chaplains. The Fifth Marines had lost a Chaplain during Operation Swift. His name was Father Capadanno. He was a very brave man. He went to help a wounded corpsman who was treating a fallen Marine during Operation Swift. The Chaplain lost his life caring for others.

He was awarded the Medal of Honor for his valor. I went to church whenever I could on the Hill.

Keeping a positive attitude is very difficult in combat. The vigor of combat was incredibly vexing on me. Like all the corpsman, I saw every injury of every Marine who was wounded in the squad I would be with. Our platoon had two corpsman but we didn't go out together unless our entire platoon went out. When I was able to hear the Chaplain speak of faith and the love of God I was encouraged and lifted up.

We got word one day that we would be leaving the Que Son Valley and Hill 51. We didn't really know where we were going. Whenever we moved out in number we either flew on choppers or we rode in the back of 6 bys (trucks). They told us the new area to where we were going was called Hoi An. It would be totally different from what we had become accustomed to. The Marines had learned to adapt to the mountains and I was slowly becoming accustomed to my new surroundings as well. But now we were moving. We would be leaving the high country and going to the lowlands. Instead of mountain trails we would be crossing rice paddies. Instead of digging into rocky earth we would be sloshing through the sometimes knee deep mud. The people in Hoi An would be different. We would have to learn how our new enemy dressed and how he lived. The friendly villagers would have to learn to trust us and we would have to establish a bond with them. We would have to learn new skills. We didn't know what awaited us. We were not fighting a conventional war. Our enemies were farmers by day and assassins by night. We would have to adapt.

Chapter 6

Of Swamp and Mines

"Hoi An days were long, cold, wet and filthy, often uneventful, even downright boring. Some Hoi An days, however, overflowed with blood, terror and death, and so we were very happy to learn, in late December 1967, that 1/5 would soon move north. During the monsoon months of October, November and December, 1967, a total of 23 Marines serving in 1/5 lost their lives; 12 of them were Charlie 1/5 Marines. Well over a hundred 1/5 Marines sustained serious wounds, requiring medical evacuation. Most of the wounds came at the hands of booby traps, mines, and the VC's weapon of choice, the command-detonated bomb. Although a much lower casualty rate than that which we had endured during the summer months in the Que Son Valley, the Marines of 1/5 were all happy to leave the Hoi An TAOR. We had been forced to fight a very frustrating war against an enemy who had no face. Their hit and run tactics discouraged us, and our quick reactions and firepower accounted for only about fifty confirmed enemy KIA's during our entire stay in the Hoi An TAOR."
(this information taken from 1/5 Command Chronology); (http://1-5vietnamveterans.org/15-combat-ops/)

We just packed up and left Hill 51 one day and moved our area of operation to Hoi An. Much American blood was shed in those mountains surrounding Hill 51. People protesting on the streets of our home towns had no idea of the price we were paying to defend our American way of life and for the freedom and liberty of the South Vietnamese people. We didn't have our minds on the politics back home.

Battlefield Faith

We had to focus all of our attention on our duties here, one day and one night at a time. None of us had any promise of a new day. We were thankful when we were given one. We couldn't linger on the loss of our buddies. We were not allowed that privilege. Our time was right now. What is happening right now? There is only right now.

I don't remember ever hearing any Marine saying he liked the swamps and mud of Hoi An. Most of our guys liked the mountains better. They were accustomed to that terrain and had adapted to it. They knew how to recognize the enemy better. They were acquainted with how the people dressed and acted in the mountains. Now we were here in the lowlands. We had to go to school again and learn. The people were different, the land was different. We had to adapt to how we went out and came in to our compound. Our training was on the job!

We slept in tents when we were not in the bush. Each man was responsible to make his own floor under his bunk out of pallets. After a while with every man contributing his efforts we had a pretty complete floor under us.

That's me on my bunk, Hoi An, 1967. Check out that cool floor we built and the accessories.

Loudermilk

We had hot chow when we were not in the bush also. I thought it was pretty good. We figured any time you get hot chow you better be thankful. Most of the time our meals consisted of c-rations and we ate them because that's all we had. We thought most of ours were left over from WWII. We thought the Army had better chow. They had the newer stuff. I remember scrambled eggs and spaghetti in some of the rations they shared with us at one of our outposts. But regardless of the situation and food or the lack thereof Marines always celebrate their birthday and November 10 was here.

10 November 1967
Friday

I

Dear Mother, Dad & Family,

Just a few lines to let you know everything is going fine. I have been pretty busy these past couple of days. I have taken some pictures and will send them home as soon as I can get them developed.

We had a real good meal today. It's the Marine Corps birthday. Sometimes I forget I'm even in the Navy.

Everything has been going pretty good. We went into a hostile area a couple days ago looking for an enemy antenna and blew it up & got helicopters out without any trouble. Although they were firing at some of the helicopters when we landed, the one I was on never took any incoming rounds. I praise God for watching over me.

My location

I don't remember too much about it but I did mail the menu home.

1967 USMC BIRTHDAY MENU

Battlefield Faith

COMMANDING GENERAL'S ANNIVERSARY MESSAGE

From the Founding of our Corps on 10 November 1775 to the present, the words Marine Corps have been synonymous with loyalty, courage and honor.

Loyalty, courage and honor are more than words to Marines. They are a tradition -- a tradition of action, a tradition of greatness. From the island of Guadalcanal to the Chosin Reservoir, and now in the rice paddies and jungles of Vietnam the 1st Marine Division has upheld the traditions of our Corps.

Born in a time of strife, the Corps has never lacked for men of courage. In the 192nd year of our Corps the courage and energy of the 1st Marine Division is now channeled toward one goal -- freedom from Communism for the people of South Vietnam.

DONN J. ROBERTSON
Major General, U.S. Marine Corps
Commanding General
1st Marine Division (Rein), FMF

192nd
Anniversary
Marine Corps Birthday Menu

Chilled Tomato Juice

Beef Noodle Soup   *Shrimp Cocktail*
Crackers

Grilled Steaks

Sauteed Onions   *Fried Mushrooms*

French Fried Potatoes

Tossed Green Salad
French Dressing

Relish Tray   *Olives*

Mixed Nuts   *Hard Candy*

Anniversary Cake   *Ice Cream*

Hot Coffee   *Milk*   *Iced Beverages*

Our men had built sand bag walls around our perimeter at the outpost in Hoi An and we continued to keep up the maintenance on them. Wire was also in place to deter the Vietcong and provide us with a more secure barrier. We had a makeshift shower but like most of the guys I never had the luxury of using it once. I was always busy. I didn't have too many days off. We bathed in the rivers or waterfalls whenever we could or when it rained. Staying clean and staying healthy was important. You watched what you ate and what you drank. I always suggested a halazone (bleach) tablet in every canteen. The dirtier the water the more tablets we had to use. More than one Marine told me at times while they had been on patrol after being without water for a while they were so thirsty when they found it they just swallowed the pill and drank the water. I never did that. I never had dysentery and I only remember one Marine in our platoon who did during my tour of duty. I medevaced him.

On one of our first patrols here we walked into an area where the ground felt peculiar. We began to walk more slowly. As we proceeded the ground seemed to move under us. It was so swampy that we had to be real careful not to punch through the earth beneath our feet. We cautiously made our way out to more solid ground. We were in full battle gear and it was a scary situation. I'm thankful "Charlie" didn't show up that time. Thank God we all made it out safe.

I was part of a three day operation around November of 1967 somewhere near Hoi An. Our Platoon Sergeant, John Mullan, referred to as "Mother" by the men in our platoon, was in charge on this particular patrol. Our Lieutenant had rotated home and I don't think his replacement, Lieutenant Nick Warr, had arrived in country yet. I was still fairly new and gaining my experience and confidence every day. We left our compound at our designated time and we were heavily armed, seeking the enemy and looking for a fight! We marched a long ways. We had to cross rice paddy dikes where we had to dangerously expose ourselves for a while then on through harrowing jungle trails being ever watchful for any line strung across the trail that could be attached to a booby trap. One of the things I hated was to be dry all day and then have to cross a creek or river toward evening just before we found a position for the night. This time we were able to stay dry for just about all of the day and I thought we had it made. I'd get to spend one rare night dry but as duty would have it in the last part of our venture we had to cross a river and we all got soaking wet.

"Mother" Mullan was looking for a place for us to dig in for the night and it had to be an area we could easily defend. It wasn't long until we came upon a fairly cleared area with pine trees growing pretty abundantly. Near this area and within our range of vision was a large rice paddy. Three work weary rice farmers stood nearly side by side striking the muddy ground just below the surface of the murky water. They appeared to pay us no attention as they surreptitiously continued with their labor. They never paused but worked vigorously as we moved in. They didn't seem to look our way much. They just continued with their work as though we were not there. But apparently they did take notice of us.

It wasn't long until the sun disappeared behind the mountains and the night was upon us. It was a very dark evening. Like men who had done this many times before we hurriedly constructed our perimeter. We dug fighting holes and took our stand. I didn't dig my hole very deep because I wanted to be able to get out quickly in case I was needed during the night. Usually if I made myself comfortable that was when things got crazy and I became somewhat wary of doing that.

    I distinctly remember the stillness of the night. You couldn't hear much movement of any kind. It was nothing like the woods in Kentucky. There you can hear the crickets, the "who, who" of an owl or the whippoorwill sounding off as darkness fell. Every man was on alert. Sometimes we would take turns taking 5 but this time I don't think anyone had dozed off yet. We were all just getting situated and settling in to our surroundings when all of a sudden we heard a loud boom! Then in an instant we heard the whoosh of mortar rounds rushing through the air. With our instincts honed we knew they were coming our way. In combat you learn to recognize the sounds of the different weapons. You become able to distinguish between incoming and outgoing fire. The mortars headed our way and some of them began to hit the tops of the pine and cedar trees. There were violent explosions with flashes of bright light. The limbs of those tall trees cracked as the rounds exploded and came crashing down upon us as well as the shrapnel from the exploding shells.

    Instead of a quiet night where the only sounds breaking the silence would be the echoes of nature, we now heard boom, whoosh, crack, crash and thud breaking the stillness and creating havoc. Then another alarming sound rang out in the darkness. It was the call for help. Corpsman! Again from another area: corpsman! And still another, corpsman! I already had my unit one medical bag strapped over my shoulder and I began to move out of the safety of my fighting hole. I hastily crawled on my hands and knees to the first position where I was needed as the mortar rounds continued to explode and tree limbs and shrapnel fell everywhere. When I got to the first man I shouted, "Where are you hit? He quickly answered in a labored voice and pointed to the area of his wound. I hastily opened my medical bag and pulled out the things I needed and began to apply the necessary dressing to bandage him up. When I finished I assured him I had to see to the other wounded men but I would be back to medevac him. I then moved on to the next wounded man and on and on until I got to them all. I don't remember how many Marines I treated that night but it was several. I remember a couple of men from the Lone Star State getting hit. One man was a very big guy.

Loudermilk

When the incoming rounds ceased we reorganized and the Marines cleared an area as we radioed for a medevac chopper. I had to remember my training and place the most seriously injured men on the chopper first. We quickly and gently loaded the men onto the aircraft until it was filled to capacity. We brought the last man but they told us they couldn't take everyone. They could only take so many in order to be able to lift off safely. One Marine suffered a shrapnel wound of his leg. I remember he was very upset they would not take him. I guess he may have placed part of the blame on me but I had to remember my triage training and transport the most seriously injured men first. I felt very badly because they couldn't take him.

After the chopper left we went back to our posts. I don't think any of us got any sleep that night. We jumped at every sound. We didn't know if another barrage of mortars would rain down upon us or not. We were more or less out in the open with only our fighting holes for shelter. We couldn't walk away. We had no other place to go. We didn't know if the NVA or Vietcong were going to come in upon us or not. We thought this barrage might have been some type of softening up ahead of a ground troop assault. I think this was one of the most harrowing nights I had to spend in Nam. As we all made our way back to our fighting holes it seemed that each unknown noise would make us flinch. Our instincts caused us to react to the faintest sounds. Our nerves were almost spent when finally the sky began to lighten up. At long last morning came and we began look around. Tree limbs were scattered all over the place in every direction. There were holes in the ground throughout our area caused by the exploding mortar rounds. We had to put this behind us now because it was time to get organized and move out.

"Mother" Mullan had his radioman to get on the radio and after notifying our command post of our incident he got orders for us to return to our base camp. We had lost a few men. Our clothes were still wet. We were tired from our previous day's operation and most of us were glad to be heading back to regroup. Now we had to figure out how to transport our wounded man. We talked for a while and then we had a great idea. We cut some wood and constructed a makeshift stretcher with a couple of the sticks and buttoned a few utility tops from some good Marine volunteers for the cover. It was a chore to carry him but his fellow Marines were up to the task. I think our platoon sergeant secured a jeep after we neared our compound and we got him back safely. This man became a great leader of Marines. I seem to remember I thought this night of the war had been tough on Texans. More than one wounded man told me he was from the Lone Star State. In all of this confusion and desperation I had to reflect on the scripture as I now recall the following verses.

Proverbs 18:24 ... *there is a friend that sticketh closer than a brother.* (KJV)
Psalms 34:17 *The righteous* cry, and the LORD heareth, and delivereth them out of all their troubles. (KJV)

Dear Mother, Dad & Family,

Just a few lines to let you know everything is going fine and I'm in good health. I thank the Lord for helping me. He is with me every hour of every day.

When I feel bad I just recite the 23rd psalms and remember that the Lord has already said he has everything worked out for me.

We were relieved to get back to our compound where we could rest a little. We could change into some fresh, dry clothes and we had hot food there and we were thankful for it. We went out on patrols every day and ambush assignments every night and we had a rotation that accommodated the task rather than the individual. When we had leisure time we enjoyed it. I remember some guys playing horseshoes. I remember this one particular Marine from South Carolina was awesome. I watched as he threw the horseshoe and tried to figure out how he made it curve like he did. I'm still trying to figure that one out. We were really surprised when one day a Vietnamese kid came by with a couple of new guitars he wanted to sell. The guitars looked pretty good. A couple of us strummed a few cords on them. We thought there was no evidence of modern civilization in this place but here he was. I had my picture taken with him.

The kid and me with the Guitars

It seems I was in Phu Bai on Thanksgiving Day in 1967 and I was waiting in line for chow. The aroma from the mess tent was tantalizing. Everyone in line was anticipating this great meal. A hot meal beats c-rations any day and this was going to be a special one. As I stood there I looked around and saw the most welcomed site I could have seen in that foreign land. My cousin, PFC Marshall King, was walking my way with a grin on his face. As we neared one another he greeted me with, "Hey Cuz." We were so glad to see one another and it was great that it was Thanksgiving. He had joined the Marine Corps, completed his training, and had been assigned to the 5th Marines and Delta Company. Some would call it fate. Others would call it chance. I call it the hand of God. Marshall and I enjoyed our Thanksgiving together as we tried to catch up on what each of us had been doing since we last saw one another.

It's really remarkable that I had joined the Navy and Marshall the Marine Corps but now we were both assigned to the 5th Marines and it was incredible that we "just happened" to run in to one another here in southeast Asia on this particular Thanksgiving Day. We were both very thankful.

Psalms 95:2, 3 *Let us come before his presence with thanksgiving, and make a joyful noise unto him with psalms. For the LORD is a great God, and a great King above all gods.*

Battlefield Faith

28 Nov. 67 ~~Monday~~

Dear Mother, Dad & Family,

Just a few lines to let you know everything is going fine & I'm still in good health by the grace of God.

You'll never guess who I ran into yesterday. Marshall King is in my Battalion. He's in "D" Company though, but at least we're in the same battalion. I sure was surprised. I was in line for chow & he came up & said hi. That's the first time I've seen him in a year & he hasn't changed hardly a bit. I thank God that we can be together.

The other corpsman in our platoon was out with

the platoon the other night &
the radioman in front of him
stepped on a mine & killed
him.

But I know
God will bring me home
safe.

well, I guess I'll close
now but write soon.
Love,
John

P.S. Pray for me.

Battlefield Faith

My cousin, Marshall, on the left and I am on the right

    Out of all the units he could have been assigned to here he was. We were able to see one another ever once in a while and it was good knowing someone from the family was not too far away. It surely boosted our morale.
    I carried a 12 gauge shotgun on an ambush near Hoi An one night. I was issued some fleshette rounds to go with it. The squad leader for this particular night's ambush told me to go down to the armory and check it out. I did as he said. They issued me a 12 gauge pump. After getting the weapon I made my way back to where the squad was assembling. I listened as the squad leader gave us information about our objective. After hearing what we would be doing for the night we began our slow walk once again down the dusty road toward the fishing village and the beach. We passed some hooches on the way but we didn't see anyone. We began crossing an open sandy area between the hooches and the ocean where only a few small bushes were growing. You could hear the waves from the ocean gently rolling onto the beach not far from where we were walking. As we drew closer to the water we heard the crack of a carbine rifle as a sniper began shooting at us. We hit the dirt immediately. We were too far for me join in and return fire with the shotgun so I got as low as I could. I ended up on my

back and I was carrying a pack. I didn't have time to throw it off. I always kept my Unit One Medical Bag free and at my side. Red hot tracer rounds began streaking through the air and appeared like flashes of lighting making a line through the darkness and toward us. It seemed like the sniper could see us but the trajectory of his fire was just above us as a couple of Marines and I lay there on the sandy ground while we tried to get our bearings. The tracers were streaming just above my chest where I lay. We were out in the open. I felt helpless as I lay there and I tried to dig deeper into the sand with my elbows but I was as low as I could go. We were scattered out pretty evenly. The Marines just ahead of us began to return fire and the Vietcong stopped firing. We then began to move toward his direction at a rapid pace. As we drew closer to the position where we thought the firing came from we found no sign of him except for his spent cartridges so we cautiously continued our patrol toward the water.

We made our way around the fishing village and were patrolling slowly on the sand along the beach between the ocean and where the grass began to grow. Suddenly a chi-com grenade came hurling towards us. Instinctively we hit the dirt and waited for the blast. Thankfully the grenade did not explode. The squad leader yelled to me, "Open up with that shotgun, Doc and spray the area with a few of those rounds!" I moved up to the grass, fell on the ground face forward and emptied the shotgun into the brush just beyond our position. He said, "Reload and hit 'em again." I reloaded and emptied my weapon again. We ceased fire at this point and it became very still. We didn't hear the enemy run away. The only sound was the surf hitting the beach. We then moved on to our assigned ambush position. We never heard another sound that night. I don't know if my "beehive" rounds found their target or scared that agitator away. He may have had a hole to crawl into but he never bothered us again. We figured we either got him or he had never heard a shotgun before. We stayed alert though because we knew there were enemy soldiers in the area and we had come to fight. However, we had no issues the rest of the night and we all made it back safely to our compound the next morning.

In a couple of days I had to go out on another patrol. "Benny" Benware was the radioman I was walking behind this time. As we were leaving our compound I began to pray my Lord's Prayer as we continued down the road. We walked a little ways then veered off on one of the trails the villagers used. We were careful and our point man was on hyper alert. As we walked

Battlefield Faith

we passed a few hooches but we didn't notice much activity. This time the villagers had disappeared and would return after we had gotten out of sight.

Once more we began to hear the sound of the ocean waves hitting the beach as we started walking on a path that was just above a long ditch running alongside of it to our right. There were some thorny bushes growing on the sides of the ditch. In the distance and to our left we began to see some hooches but no activity. Something that resembled a pond was also in our sight and to our left. Suddenly and without warning a sniper began firing at us. A shot rang out, then another. The rounds hit the ground around me and Benny. All of us jumped into the ditch with Benny falling into the thorny bushes. We sent a fire team to flush out the sniper as the rest of the squad held our positions. We listened for any more firing and heard none and we saw our men walking back toward us. The all clear was given and we all got up and I heard Benny shout, "Ouch!" I asked, "What's wrong? Did you get hit?" He replied, "No, but I fell on some briars or something and they're stuck in my face!" I checked him out and carefully removed all of the briars I could see. Then we both gathered our gear and the squad began to move out and continue our patrol. After this we were able to finish our patrol and we returned to our base camp safely.

Dear Mother, Dad & Family,

    Just a few lines to let you know everything is going just fine.

    I know you all are praying for me because God surely was with me the other day. We were walking along a path when a sniper opened up, a shot landed just behind me and I jumped into a ditch. No one was hurt. I thank God for that and I know He's protecting me.

    I got some cookies from the Edgells and they sure were good. I believe they are really wonderful people.

    A buddie of mine has a guitar and I play it ever once in a while. We don't get a whole lot of spare time here.

    I caught up on some sleep today and I feel pretty good.

Battlefield Faith

One night I did not have to go out on ambush duty but lay resting in our tent. You never knew what was going to happen next. You could be at peace in one instance and in a firefight the next. There were no off days in Nam if you were assigned to the "grunts". The calm of the evening was broken as we heard a loud explosion and suddenly men began to scramble. In a few minutes one of our squad leaders, I believe it was Corporal Sawaya, came over and said, "Doc", a squad has been hit with a massive booby trap. They have injured men down and have radioed for assistance and we have to go and see how we can help." I said, "OK," and without hesitation I started gathering my gear which was always close by.

In just a few moments we were assembled in squad strength and on our way across our compound to the back gate. We walked as quickly as we could go while anticipating Vietcong hiding in the bushes. When we came upon the squad we realized they had been hit very badly. Many men were grievously wounded. It seemed like the whole squad was lying on the ground. There were sounds of groaning and distress. I won't go into detail of the injuries because I don't want to put it on paper but the wounds were atrocious. Exploding, hot metal fiercely flying through the air causes horrendous wounds and tears fragile human bodies in unimaginable ways.

I don't remember how many men I tried to help that night but I do recall one young Marine. I helped him to the best of my ability and tried with my upmost to comfort him. I dressed his appalling wounds while he lay there in that rice paddy. I knelt as closely as I could to him and cradled him in my arms. He was mortally wounded. I didn't feel he had much of a chance of survival so I comforted him the best as I could as I knelt there with him in the water and mud where he had fallen. He was unconscious but I prayed God help this young Marine. As I held him and witnessed his laborious breathing my heart became heavy and my grief was almost more than I could bear. I had seen so much. I had witnessed unspeakable battlefield scenes and I was not even half way through my tour. But I had to continue on. There were more wounded men to see to. Other Marines came to help and I continued on to the next man.

You can go to the movies and see what resembles a war but you don't smell the gunpowder or the sweat and blood of the wounded. You don't feel the agony or hear the wounded men's exclamations of pain. You are not part of the war on the screen. You're only a spectator of what someone has created to show you what he thinks war is like. No movie could ever extract from you the well of emotions a war invokes. As I said before "War" is a killer, a thief, a fiend that is never satisfied. The only thing that helped me retain my sanity was my faith in God. God didn't cause this war. Greedy governments did. Communists who had never known freedom and liberty invaded this country and were trying hard to defeat these people by their aggression. We were there to see they didn't and we were doing our best. We needed the support of the people of our homeland and the unrestrained leadership of our superiors.

James 4:1 From whence *come* wars and fightings among you? *come they* not hence, *even* of your lusts that war in your members?

    The Marines secured the area then cleared and created a landing zone for the medevac chopper and just as they finished we heard the rush of propeller blades cutting through the night air. As soon as the chopper landed we hurried and loaded our wounded brethren aboard the bird and they lifted off for Danang. After the chopper left we made our way back to our Charlie Company Outpost. This incident was just another occasion where I was called upon to do my best to preserve the lives of wounded Marines. The time I spent at this site went hurriedly by although the memories will never cease. When these thoughts challenge my sanity I cry, "Oh God, please help me; please resolve these disturbing intrusive thoughts for they are more than I can bear. Speak words of comfort and healing to my very soul. Help me to trust in You, In Jesus Name, Amen."
    And I remember:

Psalms 18:6 *In my distress I called upon the LORD, and cried unto my God: he heard my voice out of his temple, and my cry came before him, even into his ears.* (KJV)

    In combat you don't have the luxury of expressing your emotions. You have to confront the issue that is in front of you, make instant, difficult decisions and go on with it. After experiencing an intense situation like this one you are expected to continue with your tasks ahead. We didn't talk too much about our losses. We regretted losing our friends but we were not able to mourn our fatalities. We had a ceremony occasionally whenever time would allow but we never broke down and cried. In war you become hard, almost cold. You have inner feelings but they must stay inside. You have to be professional because a buddy's life may depend upon it.

A corpsman must treat every injury of each casualty he faces and bear the grief of every man's wound. Every one! He survives in an abnormal environment. War is abnormal! Personally witnessing human bodies disfigured by weapons of mass destruction becomes an almost "routine" however provocative experience. He must put aside his emotions. There is no one else. He must do all in his power to save a life! A corpsman sees every injury of every wounded man that situations have placed in his care. He bandages every wound. He answers every call when he is needed. He keeps his emotions concealed. He has to maintain a positive attitude in a very negative situation. A wounded man needs comfort and assurance. The corpsman must project these emotions. He must try to stabilize a weak and injured Marine. He must help him to hold on until the medevac arrives.

All of these men were corpsman, one Korean (ROC) and one South Vietnamese in middle, I am on the right. This picture was taken at our Hoi An Compound.

Loudermilk

I would write home to let my family know I was o.k. and I would sometimes tell them of some of the skirmishes I was involved in but I would never go into detail of some of the heartrending experiences I had. There were many times when I wished I had someone to confide in. I would like to have had someone to talk to when I felt I had done everything I could and still lost a man. I endured many instances of guilt feelings I wasn't competent enough to face the many challenges that came my way. All I could offer was my best and that is what I tried to do. We had each other and every one of us had a specialty. We were a team. We had confidence in each other. I was the medical man and I have to believe that I did all I could do with the bare necessities I carried in my unit one medical bag and the fundamental knowledge I acquired from my Navy training. I lost a few men but I feel that my life-saving skills were not used in vain for there were others that were saved.

I remember some of the VC suspects we captured. One in particular was a muscular man. He had long black hair by our standards that covered part of his ears and practically rested upon his shoulders. He wore an oriental cone shaped straw hat that was common in Vietnam. He wore a black long sleeved silk like shirt and black shorts. His legs were scratched apparently by the jungle bushes. He had sandals upon his feet which anyone could see were flat probably due to wearing footwear with no arch support. After his capture we tied his hands behind him for our safety and his own. If he tried something he would have been shot otherwise. We wanted to take him in. We questioned him some and he only grinned without making any reply. He either didn't understand the interpreter or didn't want to respond.

8 December '67
Friday

Dear Mother, Dad & Family,

Well, I'll write just a few lines to let you know how everything is going. I'm doing pretty good and in real good health, I thank the Lord for that.

We just got back from the field. We spent 2 nights out there. We captured 2 V.C. suspects. We were down by the ocean. (South China Sea) It sure is nice down there. I thank God that we had no trouble.

Loudermilk

Most of the men I served with were teenagers. In the movies back home the war pictures always showed older men but that's not reality. Our war was fought by teenagers. I think most of them are. Young men and women should get more credit than they do. I was 19 when I went to Vietnam and turned 20 in I Corps.

We didn't have much entertainment in the way of radio and certainly not television. Every once in a while we'd hear something over a radio someone had. Many of the men played cards which was a good past time. I learned how to play spades in Phu Bai after I was reassigned to the Regimental Aid Station. But in the bush about the only way to escape your surroundings was through reading a book and there weren't very many of them. I went out with another squad once and we had a very perplexing mission. Our mission was to look for an unexploded 500 pound bomb that one of our bombers had dropped that had not detonated. The Vietcong liked to find these. They would carefully dismantle them and use the materials they gathered to form weapons to use against us such as the booby traps that viciously killed and injured the men like we had recently experienced.

We patrolled a pretty good distance from our outpost and reconnoitered the area very carefully but didn't find the bomb. We learned we would have to spend the night so we had to find a suitable place to form our perimeter. The main squad set up in some evergreen trees. The ground was sandy there. The squad leader took me aside and told me I would have to go out as part of a three man listening post or LP. We would be staying out all night. This was the only time I was ever given that assignment. I always had my 45 but there were times when one of the squad leaders would have me go to the armory and check out an additional weapon. I don't remember the squad leader asking me to do that this time.

Here is a picture a friend took of me. The hat and M16 was his. (I used one whenever a squad leader would ask me to.) I then took a picture of him. We sent them home to our families so they could envision how we were living and surviving. This was Hoi An, our home for a few months.

Battlefield Faith

You see me dressed in our work clothes and the rifle was one of the tools of our trade.

I wasn't too happy about going out on the LP because I would be leaving the squad area where I would be needed if we came under attack. If I was needed I would have to hurriedly and cautiously make my way back to them. But I always obeyed orders and I did what I was told. In doing this I felt I was in God's will because I was doing what was asked of me. I have heard of some corpsman volunteering for point but I never did that. I knew the Marines were better trained for that. I wasn't a rifleman. I was a "Doc".

Toward evening just before dark the three of us assembled and headed out to our designated LP (listening post). I remember the mosquitoes were bad that night and it started to drizzle. Sometimes the rain in Vietnam would come down slowly and continually until you realized you were soaking wet. This was one of those occasions. The night was dark and you couldn't see very far ahead of you as we settled in. We barely spoke a word but listened intently for the Vietcong so that we could warn the rest of the squad if the enemy happened to be out making his way towards our position.

We took turns taking a snooze and soon my turn came for a little shut eye. I had a poncho that I threw over me as I laid down on the wet ground. I positioned myself on my back and I always placed my head in my helmet for a pillow when the ground was damp. It kept my head out of the mud. I only slept for a short while when one of the men awakened me. As I sat up I realized my helmet was almost full of water. I gently and carefully picked it up and poured the water out and put it on my head. I always wore my helmet in the bush even when we stopped for a break when on patrol. The rain continued to fall slowly but steadily as the dark hours of night gave way to the dawn of a new day.

We listened intently all through the night and questioned any sound we heard. We were glad to see the sun come up as we began to gather our gear for the walk back to the squad. We didn't have any enemy encounters this time but we were bombarded by pesky mosquitos and we did get soaking wet. We really didn't let it bother us. We had grown accustomed to the demands of our assignments. We waited for a short while after dawn and when we felt comfortable we began to walk back toward the rest of the squad.

We gave our report to our squad leader and then settled in with the rest of the men. After we all had our breakfast of c-rations we picked up where we left off the day before, looking for the unexploded 500 pound bomb. This time we didn't have to walk very far when we found it. I remember all the huge craters in that area that were left from the bombs that did explode. We radioed back the position of the bomb and then headed back to our base camp. I chalked my LP duties up as one more experience in the Nam! I wasn't happy about it. I was the only corpsman and this episode had taken me away from the main body of men for the night. If the squad had been attacked and men had become wounded they would not have had a corpsman. I don't remember who the squad leader was.

Treasure from Home

Periodically someone would get a package from home. If we got food most of us usually shared it. Some Marines got packages more often than others. A big thing in the '60s was "shake-a-puddin, Tang (orange juice powder) and Tabasco sauce. Often the water tasted like chlorine because we had to make it safe to drink and the Tang was great for this. The food didn't have a lot of flavor so the Tabasco helped there. And lastly the shake-a-puddin was just a welcome treat from home if you were one of the lucky guys to get some in the mail.

How I missed my Mother's banana pudding my family enjoyed on special occasions or when she just wanted to make us a treat. When we found out what she was doing in the kitchen we became excited and couldn't wait to have a dish full of that delectable dessert. We never had a birthday without her making us a cake. If we got anything it had to be a cake. Even now I must have my cake for my birthday. I don't really care if I get anything else but I want my cake.

These were some of the thoughts I reminisced about in my rare quiet times however I was usually so tired and so busy that I couldn't enjoy this luxury but it was comforting to get away from combat for just a little while even if it was just mentally.

There were a few books available for us to read and pass along. I found great comfort in reading one entitled "World Aflame" someone had finished and gave it to me. It was written by Reverend Billy Graham. I was surprised to see it here right in the middle of this Southeast Asian war. I read it every chance I got until I finished it.

Another book I read was "The Robe". At first I thought I wouldn't have time to read it through because it had over 500 pages but I opened it up every chance I got and before too long I finished it. It too was an escape for me and it got my mind off of the traumatic scenes I was part of on a daily basis.

Marine A.J. Shearouse on left, I'm on the right.

11 December '67

Dear ~~Mother~~ Dad & Family,

Well, just a few lines to let you know everything is going fine and I'm in good health. The Lord is still with me, helping me each day.

The news is that we are moving about 12 miles north of DaNang. We are supposed to set up a base camp in an unsecured area.

It's raining here now almost every day. Its pretty hard to keep dry. I want you all to take some of my money and buy me a green wet suit with a hood

> Don't get a rubber one, they split too easily. Get one made out of some other kind of material and send it as fast as you can.
>
> I'm reading a book by Billy Graham called "World Aflame." It describes the world situation pretty good.
>
> Well, tell everyone I said hello and write soon.
>
> Love,
> John
>
> P.S. Pray for me.

I remember my Mother sending me some homemade peanut butter fudge once and when I opened the package it was just crumbs. It didn't matter. It was a taste from home. I shared it with the guys and it was quickly gone. I was glad to share because each of my buddies would do the same when they got a package from home. The peanut butter candy was something from the hands of my Mother and it meant a lot to me and also to the other men. These were tough men and I was becoming tough with them. Through all the bitterness of war and all the eventful skirmishes we had experienced, through all the suffering we had endured this small package from home seemed to overpower it all. It was a peaceful reminder that things will get better. We often thought as each day passed that we were just one more day closer to seeing home once again. Thanks to all the Moms who sent these loving gifts our way. Whenever we did get a package it was an instant morale booster. Letters from home were always important to us but during the holidays they were especially cherished. A note from home let us know we were not forgotten and the home fires were still burning.

Chapter 7

Three Walk Away

During this reporting period, the enemy continued his sniping/harassment of patrols, the emplacement of booby traps, mines, punji pits and the maintenance of fixed defenses in the vicinity of selected hamlets. Two significant enemy actions were initiated during the month in the Hoi An TAOR. On 9 December the 6th RD Team was ambushed by an estimated 30 VC; simultaneously CAP 6 received small arms fire and approximately 6 hand grenades were thrown into the CAP CP. On 11 December Company B received 5-8 mortar rounds and small arms fire while settling into assigned night positions. The majority of enemy initiated incidents by individuals or small groups took place in the northwestern quadrant of the 1st Battalion, 5th Marines TAOR. These contacts were usually followed by a withdrawal through previously prepared AP/mines and booby traps. Informant reports received indicated platoon/company size units operated in the northeastern quadrant of the TAOR. No contacts this size, however, were encountered by patrols. Ample evidence was found by scouts and patrols of tunnels, caves, rice caches, trench lines and fighting holes which were recently improved. In addition to 4 local guerrillas apprehended in this sector, A VC nurse was also captured and the body of 1 NVA KIA was recovered. In contrast to the high occurrence of enemy initiated activity in the northwestern sector of the 1st Battalion TAOR, in the northeastern sectors of the TAOR, engagements were about 50 percent or more, initiated by friendly forces.
(this information taken from 1/5 Command Chronology)"; (http://1-5vietnamveterans.org/15-combat-ops/)

Judges 20:29 *And Israel set liers in wait round about Gibeah.* (KJV)

A few days and nights passed and I was getting my gear ready for another ambush. Ambushes were nothing new. They were ancient warfare methods. The above scripture relates an early ambush that took place hundreds of years ago and it was used very effectively. Just about every army on earth employs them. I would be going out with another squad in the rotation this time. Some remember different numbers of men that went out that night but I remember 13 men that assembled. All thirteen men gathered for a briefing before we headed out. Included in the group was one squad leader, one radioman, one corpsman (me), three men on the machine gun team, one man carrying a law (rocket launcher) and six riflemen.

I remember Eddie Jackson., a rifleman. He was a soft spoken muscularly athletic young black Marine from Florida. He was very agile and a great boxer. He showed me a few good moves. He was quick and strong. I think it was he that talked about being a tailor when he got home. Pierson was his friend, a rifleman, who was also athletic. He was a white fellow from the Midwest. I remember what Pierson said to me once. He said, "If I'm going to get it I hope it's before I have to hump all of these hills." They called themselves, "the Deuce". They were a fantastic duo. They were awesome combatants. These two men would be walking ahead of Sawaya in the formation.

Our squad leader, Robert Sawaya, was a westerner. He was a very intelligent man with some college, maybe a degree. He was a tall, lanky sophisticated gentleman. If you had a question you could get an answer from him. All of the men of the platoon respected him. He was the kind of guy you would like to be around. I never heard him utter a curse word. He was a teacher, a big brother. I remember he just got a small Christmas tree in the mail from home and he had set it out on a small table in our tent for all of us to see. It was a reminder of home and the special time of year we enjoyed with our families. It was very considerate of his family to send him that tree. It reminded all of us of our homes at this time of year. Our squad leader would be walking two men in front of me. Jack Michaux, a rifleman was a new man and was our rear security that night and the last man in the column. He was from North Carolina. I talked with him some when he was first assigned to us. He had a good personality and I think we could have been great friends back home. He grew up in NASCAR country. Charles "Irish" McShane, a machine gunner, from Pennsylvania, who was also fairly new, would be walking a few men behind me and finally me, from Kentucky. I would be just behind our radioman. I don't remember all of the other men too well. I only recall their faces and voices. I remember some of the times we talked of home and friends and the times we laughed.

  Each of us had our personal preparation to do. While the Marines were assembling their weapons I had to make sure my medical gear was in order. I had a medical bag, a "unit one" and I knew where everything was in it. I had a place for everything and everything in its place. When we were all ready we began to move out.

  It was dark as we left our compound. As we stepped out of the gate I immediately began to recite The Lord's Prayer. "The Lord is My Shepherd…" as we moved slowly down that dusty Hoi An road. The night was calm. A slight breeze was gently passing over us. We fell into our positions in our staggered column as we continued slowly down the road. I noticed the rice paddies on each side of us. Nothing seemed out of the ordinary. You could hear the sound of our boots as we touched our feet to the firm ground beneath our steps. We didn't make any unnecessary noise as we walked. We all looked around as we continued. We were always vigilant. Each man knew his job from the point man who led our way, to the squad leader directing our journey, to the radioman standing at the ready, to the machine gun team near the center of the column, and on pass the corpsman, the rocket man, the riflemen and finally to the rear security man.

  As we walked nothing seemed out of the ordinary when all of a sudden it happened. I heard the loudest noise I had ever experienced in my life. The impact was unimaginable! A tremendous force seemed to lift me up, fling me backward and then to the ground! BOOOOOMMMMMMMM, WHOOOOOSSSSHHH, THUUUDDDDDDDDDD…… and then silence. I literally saw the radioman in front of me get lifted up and hurled through the air toward me as I went down. That's all I remember. The next thing I remember is I found myself lying on my back on the ground. I slowly sit up and listened for someone to say something. Everyone was down! No sound was heard. There was only silence. I thought I was the only one alive. I had to think fast. My ears were ringing, dust filled my nostrils and my head was aching. I never even bothered to check to see if I was injured. My only thought was to go and help my brothers, the injured Marines. I got up, gathered my "unit one" medical bag and ran to Jackson, the point man. All of the Marines ahead of me were lying motionless on the ground as I passed them. None of them were moving. I hurried and made it to the point man. I saw that he had been killed instantly. Without hesitation and instinctively I grabbed his M16, set it on fully automatic, and emptied his magazine into the tree line on his side of the road. I then laid the weapon back in its place and quickly rushed on to Pierson, the next man. I was hoping he would be alive but to my bewilderment he also had been instantly killed. Again and instinctively I reached for his weapon and emptied it on fully automatic into the area on the other side of the road where my friend lay. I wanted the enemy to know he hadn't killed us all. I feared the Viet Cong would rush in if they thought they had hurt us badly.

    I got back to Corporal Sawaya, our squad leader. He had been carrying extra ammunition and grenades in his pockets and some of it had exploded. He was critically wounded and his uniform was bloody and in shreds but he was still alive. I bandaged his wounds as best I could and let him know I was there to help him. He had an M79 and he was still clutching it as I recall. I left the weapon with him and I didn't fire it but moved on down the column and to the other side of the road to the next man, our radioman. He too was lying on the ground. I immediately saw that his jaw was broken and out of place but he was conscious. I carefully positioned a battle dressing on him and bandaged it tightly and after that I checked for more injuries and discovered that he had a perforated abdominal wound. I grabbed his canteen and wet a new battle dressing that I pulled from my unit one medical bag. I bandaged him, calmly spoke to him and tried to reassure him as best I could and then I hurriedly moved on to the next man, again across the road. He had been assigned as my body guard for that night. Earlier in the week I had placed him on light duty for three days and had just taken him off the list. This was his first duty out and now he lay mangled on that dusty road far away from home. He was conscious as he lay there groaning. I softly spoke to him and tried to reassure him like the other men I was treating. He responded in an almost whisper as I began to check him out and then I realized that he too had a perforated abdominal wound which I bandaged as I had the radioman. After applying the dressing I checked him out further and saw that he had a fractured femur. I had to be careful. I did the best I could under these conditions and I bandaged his wounds. Then I told him I had to move on and check out the other wounded men but I would be back and then I resumed my challenging task and on to the next man.

Battlefield Faith

As I moved on through the column to my shock I realized that some of the men had been killed instantly. I finally got to the machine gun team leader. He too had a fractured femur. He was conscious as he lay there on his back grasping his M60 machine gun. He was totally incapacitated. As I began to treat his horrific injuries I began to hear someone whispering farther back. It was then I realized that there were other survivors. One of these men, a machine gunner, Charles "Irish" McShane was wounded but able to help me. I quickly moved on treating each man as best I could until I made it to the last man in the column, a rifleman, Jack Michaux. He was also injured but able to help too. It seemed like everyone was splattered with blood, whether his own or another Marines.

I think both of these men were fairly new at this point and they began to ask what we should do. They were skillfully trained and highly efficient Marines. Their infantry expertise far exceeded my own. I was the senior man but I was the "Doc". They were the Marines. All I could offer in the area of combat leadership was my "on the job" training I had received in the past few months I had spent with all of the squads I had gone out with. These young Marines only needed a little direction. I respect them for considering my bit of experience I had and I told Jack to get on the radio and, "get us some help out here!" I told "Irish" to set up that M60 machine gun and spray the area around us. I was hoping that this would deter the enemy from coming in on us and hopefully they would not ascertain our incredible lack of able men.

As they set us up some security and called for help I went back to my duties of treating the injured men. It seemed like a long time but in actuality our help arrived quickly. However, as we three men worked together to hold on until help arrived I heard Jack talking on the radio and I heard the unmistakable sound of "Irish" on the M60 as he kept the enemy at bay. Then to our relief I heard the sound of the boots of anxious Marines coming to our rescue. I remember "Mother" Mullan leading the reactionary force to our rescue. They were such a welcome sight. Several corpsmen arrived with them. We all went about our duties giving aid to our injured brothers. As our work continued the Marines provided security as the corpsman worked trying to save the lives of the wounded men. A landing zone was created while we continued to try and keep our brothers alive until a medevac chopper could carry them to safety. I can't remember how many choppers came that night but I do know that the killed and injured men were taken and we three, the only survivors of this squad walked back with the other Marines to our outpost. I remember only three men out of thirteen walking back that night, Myself, Charles "Irish" McShane and Jack Michaux!

When we got back to our area I went to my tent and started putting my gear away. My ears were still ringing. I couldn't help but notice that lonely little Christmas tree sitting near our squad leader's cot. Squad Leader Mike Larson, a well-respected and seasoned Marine, came over to talk to me. Mike's Dad had been a Marine and Mike wore his salty (seasoned) hat whenever we were at our compound. I felt so bad that we lost Robert. I felt he and Mike were good friends. I was so shook up and Mike could see I needed a friend and some words of encouragement. Mike spoke some heartening words to me. After I stowed my gear away we walked outside the tent and our conversation continued for quite a while. Mike was an inspirational leader of Marines. His words were very comforting to me.

We were interrupted when our Platoon Sergeant came over and said the C.O. wanted to see me in his tent. "Mother" Mullan and I immediately began walking over and talked a little on the way. When we got there Captain Burrow asked me about the incident. He talked to me informally. He asked, "Doc, are you wounded?" I answered, "I don't think so Sir." He said, "Staff Sergeant, check him out, he has to be wounded!" He replied, "Yes Sir." It was then I looked down and noticed I had tears in my trouser legs. He checked me out and said, "Sir, I don't see any wounds." Captain Burrow said, "Have him unloose his trouser legs." We always tied our trouser legs at the boot to keep the bugs and whatever out.

I began to untie the first trouser leg and when I loosened it small jagged pieces of shrapnel fell to the wooden floor with a plink, plink, plink. I untied the other trouser leg and again small bits and pieces of sharp jagged shrapnel fell to the floor. They exclaimed, "Doc, you have to be hit." They then had me to unloose my belt so they could check for wounds on my legs. They looked closely and didn't find any. We all felt like it was a miracle that I had been so close to the explosion and my clothes were torn by the blast and I had no apparent injuries. I know I was knocked down by the horrendous impact of the detonation of the booby trap and when I came to myself my ears were ringing. I feel I was unconscious for a few moments but no one could verify this because every man on the road was either killed or wounded.

Thirteen men went out and only three returned whole. The rest were either killed or severely wounded. I had my little New Testament in its place in the vest pocket of my flak jacket that night. One of the teens at our church, Sandy Spiegel, had given my Mother a handkerchief to send me that the teens and members of our church had anointed with oil and prayed over concerning my safety and I was carrying it also.

Act 19:11, 12 *Now God worked unusual miracles by the hands of Paul, so that even handkerchiefs or aprons were brought from his body to the sick, and the diseases left them and the evil spirits went out of them.* (KJV)

It gave me a sense of comfort knowing I had something from home that my family and dear friends thought so much of me and had so much faith in GOD that they would think of me in this way. Their gift from home strengthened me as I went about my duties and I believe God honors our prayers and faith in Him. I can't tell you why some good men die while others walk away. All I can say is I always prayed and put my trust in God.

Psalms 119:114 *Thou art my hiding place and my shield: I hope in thy word.* (KJV)

The scripture above from the book of Acts speaks of God working unusual miracles by the hands of Paul the Apostle. I feel God is still working miracles through His Church. God indeed worked a miracle that night in December on that lonely road in South Vietnam for me. I have often wondered if God had sent an angel that night to walk before me or if somehow He sent His Spirit to form an invisible shield for me. I don't know how God did it but it was a miracle. Some of the men thought I was a little beyond normal to survive such a blast when all the men around me were either killed or severely wounded. Sometimes I daydream about God allowing me to see what happened that night in a dream. I don't know how God did it but I am here to witness He did perform an unusual miracle for me. The man of flesh that I am would cause me to have guilt; the spirit man within me gives God praise!

The next morning I wrote a letter home and described the incident to my family. I wanted them to know how their prayers were answered. I could only imagine how difficult these times were for them going through each day periodically thinking of me and wondering how I was making it.

16 December '67

Dear Mother, Dad & Family,

It is by the Grace of God that I can write to you this morning. A thing happened last night that I wish I could forget.

We were ~~on~~ going to our ambush position down the road when the "gooks" set off a mine. (hand detonated) Two men in front of me were ~~killed,~~ and wounded bad, and 1 killed behind me and several more wounded. The only thing I got was a little shook up and a hole in my trousers made by a piece of schrapnel

I had just received that hankerchief that was annointed for me and was carrying it & a new testament when this happened. I thank God with all my heart for protecting me.

I'm feeling fine this morning except my ears still ring a little bit. I had 3 other corpsmen & the senior corpsman helping me patch the men up & a helicopter came & got them & took them to the hospital in Da Nang.

Well, tell everyone I'm O.K. and keep praying for me & I'll be home safe soon. Love
John

Battlefield Faith

Again, I don't know why some men live and some men die but for myself I gave thanks to God for His Divine Hand of Protection that night. I feel we will see our brothers again one day on the other side.

The events of this night are a reality to many of our warriors that have gone to do battle on foreign soil to preserve our American Way of Life. They live with these memories every day. They are haunted in their dreams at night and bothered by intrusive memories during their waking hours. They deserve our honor and respect. These Marines volunteered for service and proudly answered the call of their country when they were needed. I am proud to be an American and proud to have represented my country with these valiant men.

Captain Burrow, Lieutenant Nick Warr, Staff Sergeant John Mullan and Marine Machine Gunner Charles McShane gave their affidavit of their memories of that night and Nick put me in for a Bronze Star with Valor due to Charles "Irish" McShane's testimony. I was humbled when I received this honorable award at The Marine Corps League in Louisville, Kentucky approximately 49 years after this event. The Mayor of Louisville declared November 6, 2016 as "John Loudermilk Day". The Lieutenant Governor presented me with the "Kentucky Colonel" Award signed by Governor Matt Bevin. I got a kiss and hug from Miss America, Heather French Henry, and I was awarded "Kentucky Admiral" because of my outdoor activity here in Kentucky. Marines from two different Marine Corps Leagues were represented at the presentation as well as a Marine Corps ROTC Color Guard from Fern Creek High School in Jefferson County, Ky.

This would not be the last time Charlie "Irish" McShane and I and the rest of our Marines would see action. There would be a place in our future called Hue City where some of the bloodiest fighting of the war would take place.

The following photo was taken of a memorial we had for our fallen brothers. Some of the men were missing due to their job assignments. Some were on patrol or sentry duty. That is our Commanding Officer, Captain Burrow addressing us. It was a very solemn affair.

Christmas Eve 1967

We were somewhere deep in our area of operation on Christmas Day of 1967. There were no Christmas Trees with brilliant flashing lights, no holiday cheer and laughter. There was no aroma of Christmas Dinner cooking in the kitchen. Family voices were not heard. We had our duty to our country to perform today. I don't remember anything special occurring. I seem to recall we had some hot chow on Christmas Day though.

Battlefield Faith

Christmas card 1967

Glory to God in high heaven,
and on earth peace among men of good will.
Luke 2, 14

Vinh danh Thiên Chúa trên các tầng trời. –
Và bình an dưới thế cho người thiện tâm. –

SEASONS GREETINGS

To Mother, Dad & Family,

Love,
John

1ST MARINE DIVISION (REIN) FMF
CHRISTMAS 1967, VIETNAM

When the day began to come to a close it was my turn for ambush duty. I gathered my gear together like the other men and proceeded to join them at our designated spot. This night was just like all the others. We ran so many patrols and ambushes that the routine was almost automatic. Every one of us always carried a poncho. It was part of our standard gear and you never knew when it was going to rain especially during certain times of the year. I don't remember the particular months when we had monsoons but when they arrived the rain seemed like it would never end. It wasn't raining this time as we began our careful walk to our ambush position. Like always we were constantly on the alert for the enemy. Everyone had his eyes peeled for anything unusual. All in all it was a pretty quiet night. On this occasion we had been assigned to a sandy area but there was often a swamp somewhere and you never knew where the enemy might pop out of the bushes.

    We carefully trudged on and finally after meandering our way through the bush we made it to our designated location. After we checked out the area we all began to find our places where we would settle in for the night. The claymores were placed in position and our weapons were locked and loaded. We would be vigilant and watch and listen for any activity. The radioman would answer any calls by clicking his handset. We tried to get as comfortable as we could under the circumstances. Sometimes we would allow some men to take a nap while the others would stay on alert. I was very fortunate compared to some of the others. I didn't have to stand radio watch but sometimes I would take a turn so the others could get some needed rest.

    During the night when it came to my turn to try to catch a couple of winks I heard this irritating buzzing near my ears. I slapped at the air and the buzzing seemed to stop just for a while then it returned. I had been careful before I left our outpost and rubbed insect repellant on my visible skin areas as I did on most nights like this. It didn't matter to this insect! He was either desperate for a hot meal or just bent on worrying me for the night. I couldn't make any unnecessary noise so I didn't slap very loudly so the only thing I could do was to get my poncho and cover up head to toe. I always used my helmet for my pillow whenever I could. It kept my head off of the ground. So that's what I did.

    I found myself lying on my back with my unit one (medical bag) by my side. My 45 was on my right hip and I had my head resting in my helmet. Then I struggled to maneuver my poncho over myself as best I could while trying to make as little noise as possible. After I was all covered up I thought this was going to be good. All was silent for a little while and I began to doze off. Then all of a sudden I heard it again. Buzzzzzzzzzz, buzzzzzzzzzzzzz, buzzzzzzzzzzzz. This mosquito was persistent. I don't think he left all night. He wouldn't stop. Buzz, buzz, buzz all night long. I think he was still buzzing as the sun began rise.

Battlefield Faith

We didn't have any encounters with the enemy that night but I had a foe that "bugged" me all night long. I don't think I'll ever forget it. I was so glad when this night was over. As we moved out we began to realize it was Christmas Day. Some of the men got some small mementos from home to remind them it was the Christmas season. It was difficult for us to appreciate the day because of all the horrendous experiences we had encountered in just the past few days and weeks. But it was Christmas. I remember getting a card that we could sign and send home to let the family know we were doing alright. The card said, "Peace on earth!" I thought without having the Spirit of God in your soul it would be nearly impossible to have peace in such a place as this. I was very thankful that as a young man I had accepted Christ in my life and I had that peace that passes all understanding abiding inside of me.

Philippians 4:7 *and the peace of God, which surpasses all understanding, will guard your hearts and minds through Christ Jesus.* (KJV)

As I thought about this special day I remembered the Christmas Story from the book of Luke:

Luke 2:1-7 *And it came to pass in those days that a decree went out from Caesar Augustus that all the world should be registered. This census first took place while Quirinius was governing Syria. So all went to be registered, everyone to his own city.*
Joseph also went up from Galilee, out of the city of Nazareth, into Judea, to the city of David, which is called Bethlehem, because he was of the house and lineage of David, to be registered with Mary, his betrothed wife, who was with child. So it was, that while they were there, the days were completed for her to be delivered. And she brought forth her firstborn Son, and wrapped Him in swaddling cloths, and laid Him in a manger, because there was no room for them in the inn. (KJV)

With these thoughts in my heart I tried my best to seek the peace of God and distance myself from the memory of that horrific experience on that dusty road in Hoi An, South Vietnam.

Chapter 8

A Man's Worth

"Since the Battalion's displacement to the new area of operations in Phu Loc (ZC 079989), on 23 December 1967, seven instances of contact/sightings of the enemy by battalion patrols are recorded. Three enemy mortar missions have been fired on platoon patrols and two sniper incidents have occurred. Two booby trap incidents were recorded when members of patrols unwittingly detonated one buried, pressure detonating box type mine and one M-26 grenade rigged with a trip wire. On 24 December 1967 8 VC with weapons were sighted and fired upon by the Battalion combat outpost while the enemy attempted to dig in on the forward slope of a hill in the vicinity of the Battalion Assembly Area..." (this information taken from 1/5 Command Chronology, December 1967)

The ROCs (Korean Marines) showed up one day after we got the word that we would be moving out of Hoi An. I didn't know anyone who was going to miss this place. All I remember is that an awesome number of Marines did a lot of sacrificing here. We never learned to trust the locals. They pretended to be our friends during daylight hours and could easily lay a booby trap out for us at night. We were there to help them to have a better life. We came to rid them of the scourge of communism that had infiltrated their community. We wanted to help them gain their freedom to be able to live the life they chose. But we learned we had to be on alert each time we left our base camp. The people would often grin as we passed through their villages and we would wonder what they were thinking. It was difficult to attempt to communicate with most of them. We were ready for the move when we got the word.

Here are a couple pictures of the Korean Marines relieving us at Hoi An, 1967.

That's Marine Robert Lattimer in that cool hat.

Finally we could say goodbye to the mud, the swamps and the booby traps. We were headed back toward the mountains. Other writers have given a much more detailed historical account than I ever could. My story is my personal experiences and how I was able to render aid to my wounded Marines here. When we were transferred to new areas we had to learn new rules. Corpsmen had to think of possible medical problems that may arise. Would the water be good in our new home? Will we be able to get the supplies we will need when we need them? Actually I never had any problems getting my medical supplies and I never had to worry about any Marine taking any of my supplies. I could leave my Unit One medical bag on my rack with morphine in it and no one would bother it. It would be in the same place where I left it when I returned. The Marines respected that bag as I did for it contained the medical tools I used daily.

Battlefield Faith

Dear Mother, Dad & Family,

Well, just a few lines to let you know everything is going alright.

We went on a patrol today and everything was OK, until we got back to our area. We were 100 yards from our perimeter and our point man led us into our own minefield. We all made it out safely and I praise God for helping us. I know he has his hand upon me.

Well, they're trying to make situations better now. We have a place where we can buy cokes and now we also have a movie at night. Things are looking up.

Well, I'll close now but write soon.

Love,
John

P.S. Pray for me

(Also, start numbering your letters) I've only received 1

I don't remember exactly where that mine field was I described in this letter but I place the letter here just to show you never know what one day or the next will bring in combat.

Somewhere on a hill in South Vietnam late in the year of 1967 I remember an operation I was part of. I don't remember much of the details of where we were. I do recall that I was sent with one of the squads of 1st Platoon to a hill where a few men or all of Delta Company was supplying security for some artillery. I think it was near Danang. They had been hit by incoming mortars a little while before we had arrived and were still cleaning up. I was hoping to see my cousin, Marshall King, since he was assigned to Delta and this gave me a great opportunity for a short visit.

After asking around I was told where his tent was located and found it without much hassle. When I first saw the tent I guess I exclaimed, "Oh God!", because the tent on his side was torn into shreds by shrapnel. I walked inside and his cot had been hit too. A camera which I had loaned him a few weeks before was lying on the cot busted. The wooden frame of his cot was now splinters and the canvas was full of holes. One of the Marines in the tent came over and as we talked he told me Marshall was out on patrol when the incoming mortar round had hit. I didn't get to see my cousin this time but at least I knew he was still alright.

Proverbs 18:10 *The name of the LORD is a strong tower: the righteous runneth into it, and is safe.* (KJV)

I remember the steep incline of that mountain where they were set up. We were out all night later on ambush and had taken our positions spread out on one of the peaks. We took incoming small arms fire just before dark and I began running down the jagged path to answer the call of "corpsman". I ran so fast I tripped a wire that someone later said was attached to a Chicom (Chinese Communist) Grenade. There was an explosion but the grenade missed me. I guessed I was moving pretty quickly. Thank God.

I don't imagine I thought about being hungry too much with everything else on my mind but like everyone else I just was. And I can relate with the many articles I have read that have stated, "We were always hungry!" That night wasn't any different. I don't remember eating anything that night and we didn't have anything put away for breakfast.

Battlefield Faith

Often we would find something to eat in the many villages we passed through. Sometimes a Mama San would fix us something hot and we would pay her for it. Other times we would find bananas but there were no bananas or other hot chow that night. I remember the next morning sitting in the back of a 6 by (truck) with the rest of the squad parked almost in front of a mess tent. At first glance we noticed the mess tent but as we looked around we saw that just a few feet away were three body bags that hadn't been flown out yet. "What an ominous site," I thought. It was a shame those brave men had to lie there just inches away from their buddies who had undoubtedly fought in the same skirmish these men had died in. We could relate wholeheartedly to the Marines who stood watch over them. We glanced at each other but no one spoke a word. No word was needed. We all knew where we stood.

Our thoughts were interrupted suddenly when one of the mess men came over to where we were parked and told us they didn't have any extra food for us but he did bring out a very large can of cherry preserves. Most of us carried a plastic spoon in our pockets. Someone opened the can with his "p38", a handy little can opener each of us carried, and each man took some and passed it around. We were glad to have it. At least we didn't go hungry. Although it was nothing but a can of jelly (cherry preserves to be exact)! Think about it. We had come a long ways to support our fellow Marines. We had been out on ambush all night long while encountering the enemy in a fire fight that night. We had kept ourselves together through it all making it nothing more than a typical day at work for Marine and corpsman. And here we were. We didn't think about the philosophy of it all. We were just glad to have the "jelly"!

I don't remember too much about Phu Loc six but we moved there after Christmas. We left "booby trap city" where we lost some dear friends that we shall never forget. Most of them were teenagers. Their stories live on through us who share it.

I remember digging in at Phu Loc and it was very difficult. We had become used to lowland sand and now we had mountainous rocks. The ground was filled with them and we had a very difficult time digging the trenches. I have posted here a picture of my friend and corpsman, Paul Glass, showing just how big a job it was to dig in this ground. He was from Arkansas and friendly to all.

Corpsman Paul Glass (with pick) from Arkansas and Marines digging in

I had another corpsman friend whose name was Leonard Chesley. He was a good Christian young man. He was answering the call of help one night and was trying to get there as quickly as he could. From what I remember he got into a jeep to tend to a severely wounded Marine who had performed an act of incredible bravery when he threw himself onto a grenade that was thrown into where he and his men had been positioned. It was reported that they couldn't get a chopper in to the area where they were so they had to drive the injured man to Phu Bai and then transport this Marine to Danang. The C.O. asked for volunteers.

Len was the corpsman. There was a Marine driver and a rifleman for security with them. After they had secured their patient they took off down that dark road to their destination. They hadn't gone very far when they were attacked. The enemy was waiting in ambush and heard them coming. As they neared their position they fired a rocket round at them. Doc Chesley was killed instantly as well as the driver and the security man. We'll never forget them. The original wounded man was hit again however through some miracle and Marine veracity he survived due to the efforts of help that quickly arrived from the base camp.

Len and John

I am on the left, Len is on the right. This picture was taken at Phu Loc 6 and was one of the special times that friends got to spend some leisure time together and talk about home. The NVA were amassed in those mountains behind us.

I recall another operation we were on however I don't remember too much of the particulars except that I think it was Platoon size. We were moving at our regular stride along a trail somewhere in the bush and surrounded by enemy forces as usual. We were hiking in "Charlie's" space looking eagerly for him and his buddies when a call for assistance came over our radio. "Mother" Mullan halted the column while making plans to redirect us. We were then given our orders. A village ahead of us was being overrun by the enemy and we had received the call for help. We proceeded to "force march" in full battle gear to assist them. I think the distance was 12 kilometers or about 7 miles. As our pace picked up I reminisced about our training at Camp Pendleton. The more combat I was involved in the more thankful I became of the instructors that pushed us back then. I remember one Sergeant who taught us how to throw a grenade. He was a combat veteran of Nam. He had been wounded and showed his respect for us and the job that lay ahead of us.

Well, here I was and this was for real. We were closing in on the village and we began to slow our pace. We spread out and began to carefully search the area. As we approached the hooches we saw flags that had been placed in various places all around the area. They were hanging from every hooch as high as they could place them. They were NVA flags. There were many of them. Most of us were pretty serious and didn't take any for souvenirs. There was always the danger of something being booby-trapped. To reach up and grab an enemy flag would be stupid.

I have carried the following scene in my memory since that time and now I write it here. An NVA or Viet Cong who was fluent in English had written on the side of a huge boulder near the path we had to walk down the following message: "GI Go Home! Don't 'you know that your B52s are killing innocent women and children?" More propaganda followed but I'll not attempt to place it here. These same animals destroyed a nearby harmless village murdering the innocents that lived there and had taken captives and fled as we neared their position. We all read it as we passed this confrontational thought from a brutal North Vietnamese soldier. They were the assassins as would be attested in the following weeks of the upcoming Tet Offensive. They would be the ones who would dig massive graves in Hue City to hide the bodies of the helpless and unarmed civilians they would massacre. We just got very mad when we read that. That was the propaganda that spread to the streets of our cities back home and on to the college campuses. We didn't get many newspapers. About the only one I remember seeing was the Stars and Stripes but we heard rumors from home.

We secured this area quickly as evening was drawing near and each man claimed his space for the night. As we spread out I found a place where I could easily get out and go in all the directions if I was needed during the night. The darkness was calming for a while but during the night we took some incoming small arms fire and some mortar rounds. We suffered a few casualties but I believe we wreaked havoc on "Charlie" and his pals. I tended to each injured man and then I needed to medevac my wounded

Marines so we radioed for choppers. After a brief period of waiting which seemed like an eternity while my Marines lay there in pain and bleeding the incoming message informed us there were no available choppers that could be sent. We all became irate to say the least. I have a mental blank of how this ended but I know we put forth great effort and got these men out the best way we could. I think we must have carried them out to the nearest road in the morning where vehicles met us there.

    I was so upset I felt I couldn't take anymore. There was dried blood on my hands and uniform. The smell of death and dying permeated the air. I had done all I could to help these men and get them to the safety and security of a military care facility. I felt overwhelmed. There were so many casualties and I incurred an incredible amount of stress. It was my responsibility to try and keep these men alive until they could be medevaced. I needed a break. I did all I could and I feel more could have been done. In the morning we began our long march to the nearest road. Then we had to walk back to our main area. Grunts do a lot of walking. Maybe that's why they make you walk so much in training. I left the column when we reached the main road. I told some of the men I was going to Danang to see the Bob Hope Show; after all it was close to Christmas. They said, "Doc, you might get into trouble." I was a 3rd Class Petty Officer, (same rank as a Corporal), and at that moment I didn't care if I lost all of my rank. I needed a break. Like some other guys have said, I remarked, "What are they going to do, send me to Viet Nam?"

    Here is a picture of the Bob Hope show that I took with a little Polaroid camera I had. Notice the men to the right on top of the telephone poles. (I apologize for the quality but some of my pictures had to finish my tour of duty with me.)

Bob Hope Show, 1967, Danang

There were a lot of guys there that had come to watch the show. A few of them climbed the telephone poles for a better look. I saw men from the different branches of service. Many of them were Marines. I believe we had a Marine Air Wing stationed in Danang. The Navy had a hospital there and we also had the First Medical Battalion. One of my friends whose name was Smitty was stationed there. He was from Texas. We had served together at the Naval Hospital in Subic Bay, Philippines. I saw him once when I had gone to see one of our men who had been injured in that horrible ambush in Hoi An.

Battlefield Faith

I am on the left, Smitty Is on the right holding my 45

    I saw Miss World, Raquel Welch, Les Brown and his Band of Renown and of course Bob Hope. He used cue cards extensively. There was a lot of great laughter. I really enjoyed the show. The troops had gathered in the area and many of them had been there for a very long time. I remember the long wait for the entertainers to arrive. After a while we heard the thunderous sound of choppers headed our way. I turned and looked into the sky at the sound of the almost deafening rotor blades and realized then and there that I hadn't seen that many choppers flying together like that for a very long time, if I ever had. As I watched the group of aircraft approach I was grateful to be here forgetting about where I was and the strain the battlefield had placed on me. I appreciated the contribution these talented people were making to the uplifting of our morale and I can say watching the show helped me get through the difficult memories I was confronting. Thank you Bob Hope and thanks to all the wonderful people who came to entertain and encourage us.

    After the show I had to hitch a ride back to our outpost. I was able to get several rides along the way. But the one I remember most was when an older man dressed cleanly and wearing a gentleman's straw hat who was perhaps a father and a younger woman, maybe a daughter, stopped to pick me up. They were driving a nice large truck. The kind of vehicle you would see delivering groceries to a super market back home. They didn't speak much English but we managed to understand each other. There wasn't much conversation as we rolled along. They took me a good ways up that road and finally I saw we were near my destination so I asked them to stop. I got off the truck, waved goodbye, and they smiled and then waved back. That's the last I saw of them. I made it back ok and no one asked me anything about my absence. I guess they may have known Doc needed a little time off.

> Dear Mother, Dad & Family,
>
> Just a few lines to let you know everything is going just fine & I'm in good health, and the Lord is with me.
>
> We have moved a little farther north from the last time I wrote. We are about 10-12 miles south of Phu Bai.
>
> We are just building our new area. We're the first ones here. There are a lot of mountains all around us & a road is real near.
>
> I got your letter, Ruth, and was glad you wrote. I saw Marshall a couple days ago and he said he got a letter from you too. We took some pictures together Christmas.
>
> Well, tell everyone I said hello & Pray for me
>
> Love,
> John

Then I returned to my duties and before I knew it I was out on another patrol. The war didn't stop for anyone. We were blessed when we were able to see another day.

Chapter 9

Endeavor to Persevere

A sharp rise in enemy initiated incidents to include platoon/company size engagements characterized enemy efforts during this reporting period. Between 1 January and 7 January, the enemy increased his sabotage, mining and ambush activities along Highway 1. With increased frequency the enemy, in a series coordinated incidents, successfully interdicted Highway 1 by blowing bridges during night hours, planting anti-personnel and anti-vehicular mines and with attacks against Marine engineering and mine sweep units. The enemy utilized command detonated mines in conjunction with grenades and surprise heavy automatic weapons fire. These incidents culminated with a series of coordinated attacks on the morning of 7 January, commencing at approximately 0335H the Phu Loc District Headquarters and CAP H5 (ZD 0800), CaP H6 (ZD 1400) and CaP H7 (ZD 2001) along Highway 1 were subjected to coordinated sapper and infantry assaults which the enemy supported with heavy mortar and B-40 rocket fire. Shortly thereafter the 1st Battalion, 5th Marine Command Post (ZG 076985) was subjected to heavy mortar and recoilless rifle fire. (This information taken from 1/5 Command Chronology, January 1968)

We were seeing more and more activity by the enemy. We were taking incoming mortar and artillery fire pretty often. I was one of the more fortunate men. I was usually out on patrol or ambush assignments most of the time and I was able to get away from our base camp. I don't ever remember having a meal in the mess tent. We were at a higher elevation than our previous outpost and I do remember the temperature dropping and it getting cold. At one point a heating stove was issued to each tent. The tent area may have been more comfortable but the trenches were safer. Like many of the other men I chose the trenches.

1 January 1968
"Happy New Year"

Dear Mother, Dad & Family,

I guess I'll start the New Year off right by writing you a letter. Hope everything is going fine and I'm hoping that my tour here will be over soon. I know God is with me & hears me when I pray.

We just got back from a 5-day company sweep here in the mountains. We're approx. 12 miles South of Phu Bai. It's raining here now and has been for the 5 days now. I guess the Mormons are finally here.

I just filled out a paper for a news release from the paper there in Cincinnati. I don't know if they'll print anything or not but be looking in the paper for an article. They're doing this because we moved farther north, where we are now.

Everything is going just fine here but it's a little cold & wet. See if you all can send me some instant soup (in packages). I'll write again soon.

Love,
John

Loudermilk

We were bombarded with mortars and rockets almost on schedule from the high mountain areas surrounding our outpost. One time an airstrike was called in to give us a little relief from all of the incoming fire. It was an amazing sight to see the phantom jets make their incredible maneuvers as the pilots commanded their every move. I talked to a radioman after the air strike was over and he told me the pilot said it looked like an NVA R &R area up there. They were scrambling like ants on an anthill as their mountain hideaway was attacked.

It may have been that same radioman who got a hot new record from home and played it for us on his little record player someone had sent him. It was a new hit called, "I'm a Soul Man". Someone ran an extension cord from one of the generators and we plugged the record player in. It was great to hear some music from home and we were all glad to be able to escape the stress of combat for just a little while.

I remember moving in and out of an area called Hai Van Pass. We had some bridge security duty and continued our patrols and ambushes. We did mine sweeps in just about every area we were in and I guess this was no different. I remember on New Year's Day a young boy I had befriended from a local village who was about 10 or 11, I would guess, brought me a bowl of rice with little bits of bacon on top. To Americans this may not have been much. We are used to turkey and ham dinners on our holidays but this was a special gift from his family. He said, "This is for you Doc." I was totally surprised and very thankful he had thought about me on this holiday and I appreciated the food. I had kidded around with this little guy some when we were not out in the bush and he was offering his thoughtfulness in return. Everyone else was eating c-rations but I was having a special treat from the home of a friend.

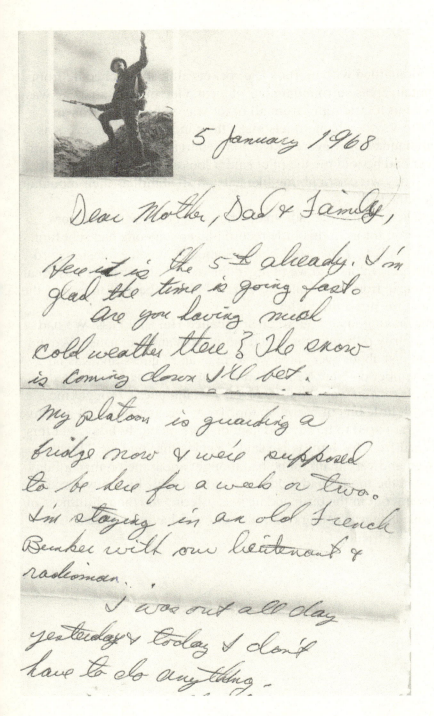

5 January 1968

Dear Mother, Dad & Family,

Here it is the 5th already. I'm glad the time is going fast.

Are you having much cold weather there? The snow is coming down I'll bet.

My platoon is guarding a bridge now & we're supposed to be here for a week or two. I'm staying in an old French Bunker with our lieutenant & radioman.

I was out all day yesterday & today I don't have to do anything.

Loudermilk

We were hit just about every day with nuisance mortar rounds. Sometimes one of the men would get a package from home with a treat inside. These times were special. Usually we would all share what we got. Quite often that nuisance crew was ready with their weapon as soon as we got comfortable. I can't remember if it was cookies this time or something else but I do remember just as we were sitting down to enjoy it we heard the sound of "bloop" and we would know a mortar round was exiting the tube and flying in our direction.

Finally we had enough of it and Nick Warr, our Lieutenant and Platoon Commander, put together a plan. He picked Corporal Ed Estes's squad for the job. And it was my turn to go out on this ambush. Nick wrote a great story of the event and called it "The Phantom Mortar Crew". We meandered pretty slowly up that mountain in the darkness of the early morning. We had to be extra careful and hold our noise down to a minimum. We wanted to get as close to the enemy as possible without them hearing us. We left what seemed like "in the middle of the night" so we would be there when "Charlie" went about his business. Ed had instructed the men not to fire until he gave the order so we were all careful as we moved along. But we had a couple of new guys with us then and they were just doing the job they were trained to do. They instinctively fired a little early as we neared our preplanned position when they heard the enemy preparing his weapon. I remember the grade where we found ourselves was very steep. The only weapon I had this time was my 45 so when they opened up I hit the dirt beside a large fallen tree and waited for when I may be needed.

Ed was just above me when he opened up with his M16 and as he fired his weapon some of the ejected casings fell down the back of my shirt. I didn't want to rise up and shake them out because I didn't know if those Vietcong were firing back or not. At this point no one had yelled for a corpsman so I just stayed put. Those rounds were extremely hot and I got a few burns but I didn't move until Eddie ordered us to proceed. When I got up a hand full of brass fell out of my shirt. That's the only time anything like that ever happened. When I told the guys they only laughed. (Lieutenant) Nick's plan worked and (Corporal) Ed's squad did an excellent job carrying it out. Nick had ordered a preplanned artillery barrage to follow our efforts that morning and the enemy was eliminated as he ran away. We weren't harassed by the mortar crew anymore. We fell back into the routine of bridge patrol and our daily patrols and nightly ambushes. We never knew what the next day or night would bring. We had to be vigilant at all times.

I wrote another letter home a few days after the last one. Like all good Mothers mine was very concerned about me but she was a praying woman. She trusted God in everything. She was a woman of faith and she believed God would bring her son safely home again. I felt that if I would have faith and agree with her that God would honor our prayers.

Mark 11:24 *Therefore I say unto you, What things soever ye desire, when ye pray, believe that ye receive them, and ye shall have them.* (KJV)

1John 5:14, 15 *And this is the confidence that we have in him, that, if we ask any thing according to his will, he heareth us:*
And if we know that he hear us, whatsoever we ask, we know that we have the petitions that we desired of him. (KJV)

Matthew 18:18, 19 *Verily I say unto you, Whatsoever ye shall bind on earth shall be bound in heaven: and whatsoever ye shall loose on earth shall be loosed in heaven.*
Again I say unto you, That if two of you shall agree on earth as touching any thing that they shall ask, it shall be done for them of my Father which is in heaven. (KJV)

Dear Mother, Dad & Family,

I thought I'd drop you all a few lines to let you know everything is going fine and the Lord is helping me every day.

I'm still out in the field from the last time I wrote. Actually, I'm not doing much at all. I sit around all day down here by the waterfall & just have / watch at night. The South China Sea you can see in the background. What we're supposed to be guarding this Pass. I praise God that we've had no trouble recently.

Well, pray for me & I'll write again soon.

Love,
John

Battlefield Faith

On various occasions we found that trying to catch a little shut eye could be easy sometimes but difficult on others. I was on an ambush one night near a trail that led nearly straight up the side of a mountain. The claymore mines had been placed in position. The watch was posted and the duty radioman was on alert. Some of us were allowed to try and catch a little sleep and then relieve those on watch. I was so exhausted that I fell asleep pretty quickly. In a short time however I was awakened when a Marine whispered, "Hey Doc, I had to wake you up because the VC could have heard you snoring for a mile." I remember being so tired. I said, Thanks." Then I told him to wake me anytime if I snored again. We each watched the others back.

I quickly went back to sleep and about dawn I woke up but the funny thing about it was most of the squad was a few feet above me on the side of that mountain. I had evidently slid down the steep slope in my sleep and a small branch shooting out of the ground had caught me. We all had a good laugh at my expense. I don't think any of this is in the official report or at least I hope it isn't. I wrote about this incident and I place it here.

The Twig and the Baby

Somewhere in Southeast Asia a seed was blown by the wind to a steep hillside alongside a mountainous trail. The yearly monsoons watered the ground profusely during rainy season and the sun beat down mercilessly the remainder of the year. Wild creatures crawled by where the seed became planted in the fertile ground and in time it sprouted. The sprout grew with the combined efforts of the sun and rain as the wind from the valley below blew up against it and made it robust. Its roots grew deep into the soil clinging to the rugged mountainside until a bush was formed. The bush was not harmed by its environment but the harshness of its surroundings gave it strength.

In another part of the world a baby was born in another mountainous region of the United States. He was the son of a coal miner. His mother had grown up in the mining camps of southeastern Kentucky. Her father was a miner. The baby's grandfathers were coal miners. They lived in an area where hard cruel work was routine. Each day the men would venture into the earth where no sunlight was seen. They had to wear lights upon their hats in order to move about and earn their living. Dedication to their families propelled them as they struggled to hack out a living. Thoughts of the father no doubt were filled with the baby's coos and laughter as he labored vigorously in the dark coal mines.

The baby grew and at the age of 17 joined the military. His uncle had been a Navy man and he had great respect for him. The baby, now a young man, was trained, then trained some more and was eventually assigned to the United States Marine Corps as a Navy Hospital corpsman. With them he went to war. Hardly a day went by without the young man caring for his wounded brethren.

The young man was expected to fulfill his duties on patrols, ambushes, convoys, morning mine sweeps, as well as tending to the sick daily. Wherever the Marines went he was to accompany them. He flew on many types of aircraft with them. He sailed on various vessels. He was accustomed to the sound of the many weapons which echoed in the war torn land. His senses were heightened. He learned to recognize and identify a number of smells, sights and sounds. Like the squirrel that scurries off or the deer that runs and leaps when it hears an unknown sound the young man became as them to survive.

On one occasion the young man, who had now earned the title "Doc", had to accompany one of the squads on a night ambush. The area where they were to go was high upon the hillside of a neighboring mountain where the enemy had been firing mortar rounds at his company. Upon arrival to the squad leaders chosen area they began to set up their claymore mines around them. The men spread out when this was done and settled in for the night. Watches were posted and soon the men were positioned for their night of vigilance.

There was no enemy encounter that night but the "Doc" was surprised when he awoke from dozing off. He had slipped down the side of the mountain from his initial position and to his amazement found himself astraddle a hedge like bush. This was the day the baby and the seedling became acquainted. The "Doc" looked down and realized how this twig of a bush kept him from falling. Had it not been for this bush he may have encountered serious injury.

But you see the baby or young man or "Doc" had a heavenly Father who planted that seed long before the two had any thought of one another. The seed had prospered and provided a safe rescue of one of God's children. The young man looked up and thanked his Heavenly Father that day for once again providing an anchor for him to hang on to. God always makes a way where there seems to be no way. He makes the impossible possible. God continued to protect this young man and steered him back safely home to his praying Mother and Father and family.

    Thank you Heavenly Father for your Divine Providential Care of those who love You and turn to You when they are in need.

Psalms 4:8 *I will both lay me down in peace, and sleep: for thou, LORD, only makest me dwell in safety.* (KJV)

11 January 1967

Dear Mother, Dad & Family,

I'm glad I finally have a chance to write and to let you know everything is just fine, the Lord is taking good care of me & I'm in excellent health.

I got some good news the other day. It seems they want to promote me to E 5, (2nd class Petty Officer) same as sergeant, in April. I'll be making more money then beside I'll get another raise for having 3 years in April 29.

I miss church & the fine meetings we used to have. I'll be glad when I can come home & hear our new pastor.

I'll be going to the aid station or the medical Bett. in Danang in a month or two.

My company & Marshall's platoon were on an operation together last week. while we were in the field our areas were mortared. I told Marshall & I know the Lord is watching us both.

Well, keep praying for me & I'll write again soon.
Love
John

Loudermilk

Here it was January 1968. I remember the hot, humid climate of Vietnam. I can't forget the torrential rains. Many times the rains fell continuously and we had to continue our mission regardless of the weather. At home my family was having cold winter weather in Cincinnati. That city was built upon the hills in southern Ohio right on the river. The snow was beautiful when it fell there. If you were looking down at the river from Mount Echo Park in Price Hill you could see the fairytale like flakes gently floating through the air and settling on the trees, hills and water below. Sometimes you would see a river barge cutting its way through the cold water as the winter mist would blow across its bow and the icy water would make a rooster tail at the stern of the vessel.

I could only dream of home here. This place was so much different. This land was challenging. The added fact that we were heavily engaged in combat with a formidable opponent just made things more difficult. In spite of our challenging circumstances we had to depend upon one another. Our very lives depended upon it.

John on right, Marine friend on left, Huey gunships in rear

Battlefield Faith

We were involved in quite a bit of action in the coming weeks. We only took one day at a time and one night at a time. The typical Marine or corpsman didn't keep any records and didn't know exactly where he was at any given moment. But things were building up. There was tension in the air. It seemed like the entire country resembled a heavily overloaded pressure cooker that was about to explode. Many of the villagers continued to show signs of distrust and uneasiness when we would pass through their areas. One of our greatest deficiencies was our lack of communication skills. We couldn't carry on a conversation with the locals we would daily come across on our patrols. Some of the Vietnamese kids picked up a little English from us. They seemed to have more confidence in us than the adults. Americans like kids and these children realized it.

We didn't know exactly how bad things were getting. We were young and highly trained for the job that consumed us daily. A large part of our training was not to ask questions. "Ours was not to question why but ours was to do or die!"

13 January 1968
Saturday

Dear Mother, Dad & Family,

I thought I'd write you a few lines to let you know everything is going just fine & the Lord is with me.

They had air strikes on top of the hill behind our area & all around.

I'm sitting in a bunker now while writting. There are a lot of guys who sleep in them & I do sometimes.

I got a Pathway & Evangel in the mail day before yesterday. I enjoy reading the articles in them.

Well, keep praying for me & I'll write again soon.

Love,
John

The 23rd Psalms became a constant companion to me as I prayed this prayer every day I was in Nam. I continued to carry my Gideon New Testament Jimmy Mathis and I got from that Chaplain some days back. I still have it. It still has a touch of sand on it from Nam. I keep it in the top drawer of my dresser and pick it up, caress it for a few moments each day, think of my brothers and what we endured together in that land so far away and gently place it back for safe keeping. It means a lot to me just to know this little Bible went through every firefight I was in. It crossed every river and rice paddy I had to trudge through. It went with me on bridge patrol, mine sweeps and convoy duty. It was in my flak jacket pocket when we were landing in hot landing zones. I found comfort having it with me and I felt a peace knowing God's Word rested over my heart in the left pocket of my flak jacket.

My Gideon New Testament

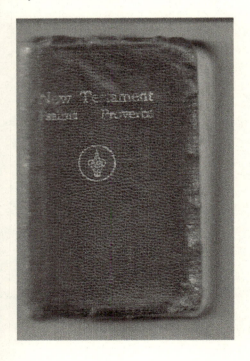

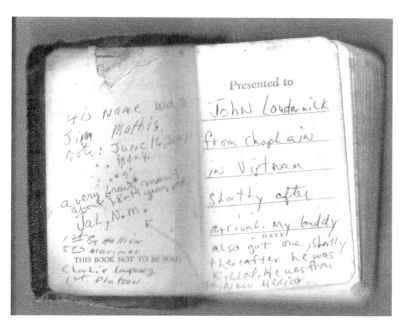

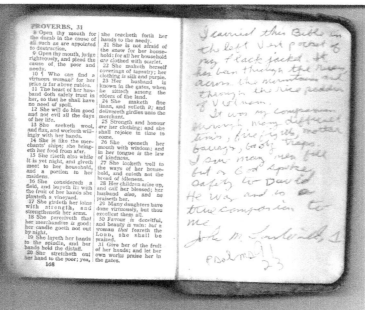

Battlefield Faith

My Mother and Dad and family, my Pastor and Wife and Church family were all praying for my safe return. I placed my trust in God to help me make it home safe but I didn't force my beliefs on anyone. I didn't play holy Joe but I was always willing to be there if someone needed me and try to answer a question to the best of my ability. Once a salty Marine whose name I forget and whose tour was getting short asked if he could throw his poncho down beside mine one night when we were out with his squad on ambush. I said sure. We had been through some tough fighting and as we were sitting there he asked me if I could do last rites. I said I was not qualified but I shared a few words of encouragement with him and I believe he felt more assured. I was there for him and I knew he was there for me.

Friday
26 January 1968

Dear Mother, Dad & Family,

Well, I thought I would drop you all a few lines to let you know that the Lord is taking care of me & I'm doing just fine.

I'm still out here on this hill with my company. We're guarding a pass until all the 1st Marine Division moves North. They're in the process now. The Army is taking over Da Nang & the Marines are going to take the North.

> *The sun is out & it's starting to get hot now. The rains are starting to cease.*

We used to talk briefly to some of the guys that passed our position near the road. Many of the drivers had painted personal names on their vehicles. Some drew colorful pictures. It was similar to the planes of World War II. They were just guys like us and like the men their same age at home. Like us they were committed to doing the best job they could until their rotation date came. That is what we all lived for. When a man "got short" he usually made himself a short timer's calendar. He would mark off the previous day as the sun rose on the next. I made such a calendar and it was thrilling to mark the days off because I knew that each mark got me closer to home.

We were glad to see the rains coming to an end for another season although we did not look forward to the heat of the rest of the year. I didn't have a favorite part of the year in Nam. I only longed for my own country, my family and my home.

We hardly ever saw a newspaper and never had any AM/FM radios. We heard "Chris Noel" every once in a while when we were in what we called "the rear" area. She was an Armed Forces radio disc jockey broadcasting from Danang I think. It was good to hear her voice over the air waves and the music from home she played. It made you think of home and how peaceful and orderly everything was when you left. It gave you somewhat of an escape from the reality of war you were facing every day and night.

I am not sure of the dates but our 1st Platoon was assigned an operation once where we had to destroy a radio tower. We boarded our #34 choppers. When we flew in these helicopters the doors were always kept open. We sat on the deck (floor) and we always had our full load of battle gear. The choppers had a pilot, co-pilot and a door gunner who maintained a belt fed M60 machine gun.

When our chopper took off we all began to think of what may lay ahead. We checked our gear as we flew and no man said a word. Then soon we reached our destination. As we were flying in we realized the LZ (landing zone) was hot. The Viet Cong or NVA soldiers were firing at us but we continued our duty bound approach. I remember the zing of the enemy rounds hitting the aircraft on one side and popping through and zinging out the other side. Our pilot was very skilled and flew in quickly and directly to our drop off point. I knew not to hesitate when the door gunner gave the order for us to exit. I realized we were not as close to the ground as we normally were apparently because of the intense incoming fire from the tree line and the village. The pilot wanted to drop us off and get out of there as quickly as he could. I was just behind one of the newer men and he paused just for a moment as we hovered at about what seemed 10 to 15 feet or so above the muddy ground. We were accustomed to jumping out at a certain level and this wasn't it.

The door gunner mumbled something and gave this man a push. He landed face down and the barrel of his M16 stuck in the mud. I jumped quickly behind him never looking back as I moved with the rest of the men toward the hooches. There were some other Marines who were just ahead of us and soon the enemy snipers weapons were silenced. They wouldn't bother anyone else with the crack, crack, crack of their carbine rifles.

"Mother" Mullan provided some steadiness as he directed our platoon through the village toward the elephant grass and the tower we were to hit. We moved cautiously through this grass expecting to see the enemy jump up at any time. There was the crack of another enemy weapon periodically but we did not let it deter us from our objective. It wasn't long before we successfully found our target. I don't remember the details but the men who were experts at their craft set their explosives and the tower was eliminated with a huge explosion. As soon as the work was done we had orders to proceed across this large open grassy field and wait at the river. The enemy could hide anywhere and be upon us in an instant. He could have devised booby traps anywhere we might walk. We were cautious as we proceeded to follow the trail our point man was marking just ahead of us.

We made it across the area without any opposition however and on to our second objective without suffering any casualties. We were supposed to call for helicopter extraction when our task was completed. It wasn't long until our radioman got a reply to his call. The word we received was that there weren't any available choppers to send for us and we had better prepare to spend the night. We began to feel a bit uneasy because we all knew we were surrounded and outnumbered. This wasn't the first time we had received a call like this.

Battlefield Faith

To our relief Phantom Jets were sent and began dropping napalm just across the river from us. The jets screamed down from the sky toward their targets getting very close to the ground then dropped their payload. Instantly the jets nosed upward and streaked into the sky as the bombs exploded in a blaze of fire and smoke. I don't see how anything could live through that. The entire area across the river was aflame.

It was growing toward evening and soon the sun would go down and we would be stuck out here with no backup. I prayed, "Oh, God, please hear my prayer. I pray that some choppers would become available and we would be able to be lifted out of here." I know I wasn't the only man praying. There were other guys who trusted in God as well as me.

We were almost past the time the choppers could be sent when we got another radio message that they were on the way. I thought, "Thank God." If we had to we would have stayed, and fought. At one point "Mother" Mullan addressed all of us and said, "If we have to stay here and we get into a firefight we will fight to the last man!" He meant it and we would have had to fight for each other.

In the distance we heard the welcoming rush of rotor blades and soon our rides were in view. I am thankful to say that we all made it out safely and lived to fight another day. As far as I can remember we had no casualties. There was a lot of relief expressed on the faces of the men as we flew away from that place. We didn't know at this point though that the biggest battle was still ahead of us.

Loudermilk

Wednesday
7 February 1968

Dear Mother, Dad, & Family,

Just a few lines to let you know that everything is going fine.

We're still in the field from the last time I wrote. I'm pretty dirty but I'm feeling pretty good.

Well if everything works out like it should (& I'm praying) I should be transferred from the field either at the end of this month or sometime next month. I hope & pray I can get transferred to Phu Bai & the Medical Battalion there. If I don't get that I'll be happy with the Battalion Aid Station.

Did you all hear about Marshall getting hit. Well, he caught a little shrapnel from

Battlefield Faith

> *an exploding rocket but he'll be O.K., so don't worry about him. (Just pray) Tell Lizzie not to worry too. Marshall sent word to me that he'll be O.K.*
>
> *Well, keep praying for me & I'll write again soon. Love, John*

I tried to write home every chance I got to stay in touch with my family and let them know how I was doing. I know it must have been difficult for them every day knowing their son was involved in a war in Southeast Asia. I remember once we didn't have any paper available to write on so they told us to cut the back off of our c-ration box and use it as a post card. We did and I remember that day very well. Many of the guys said there post card arrived to its destination but my card didn't make it.

I believe this next letter was written at Phu Loc. I had to let my folks know I was keeping the faith and doing well. Sometimes things got pretty hard and I was faced with situations out of my control. We endured hunger, thirst, fatigue, wet, cold, heat, terror, exhaustion, helplessness, anger, fear, hate. These were some of the feelings that we felt in combat. These emotions were difficult to face alone. You really can't talk to anyone about how you feel. You can't release your emotions when confronted with these thoughts. We had to be strong for one another. It helped me to know I could whisper a silent prayer to the One who could help me to bear my trials. My faith helped me to realize God was with me as I learned to trust in Him. When the sniper had me in his sights God was there. When the enemy set a booby trap along the trail and I passed by God was there. When I became stunned by the carnage of battle my God was there. I learned to trust in God and depend on my faith in Him to carry me through. Many times my faith was challenged as I beheld men horribly mutilated by modern weapons. The sounds, the smells, the vision of battle are things that are challenging to overcome after you leave the battlefield but I still have my faith in God. You never forget but with prayer they are lighter to bear.

> Dear Mother, Dad & Family,
>
> I got your letters yesterday and glad to know all is well. I'm doing real good & the Lord is with me.
>
> A couple more servicemen are getting out of the field and I guess I'll be getting out pretty soon. Pray that I will.
>
> Well, I'll close now. Write soon & pray for me.
>
> Love,
> John

Battlefield Faith

The Bible teaches that God is love. The very essence of God is love. It was because of Gods great love that He gave His Only Begotten Son that mankind may be saved and live eternally with Him.

Our God is Love but our God is also mighty, powerful and fierce in battle. His is a refuge when you need a place to run to and a helper when you feel like you can't handle any more.

Psalms 46:1 ...*God is our refuge and strength, a very present help in trouble.* (KJV)
Jeremiah 20:11 *But the LORD is with me as a mighty terrible one...* (KJV)

Dear Mother, Dad & Family,

I thought I'd drop you all a few lines to let you know everything is going just fine and the Lord is helping me.

We are still in the same place as we were the last time I wrote. (441 VAN Pass)

There was a truck that ran off of a bridge today and hurt a bunch of men.

I'm listening to some country music right now. The Osborn Brothers are singing a song called "Kentucky". It's the Grand Ol Opry on tape. It sounds pretty good.

Battlefield Faith

I always asked my family to pray for me and in doing so I know they would also pray for the men I was with. My Mother and Dad would request prayer for us at Church when they gathered for worship and many of our friends would pray for us. I know God heard those prayers. Many of us men also prayed. I prayed every day and as I said before I always prayed the 23rd Psalms when I went out.

Chapter 10

The Battle of Hue City

A very sharp rise of enemy initiated incidents to include platoon/company size engagements characterized enemy efforts early in this reporting period. At 010210H, CAP H5 and the Battalion Assembly Area came under heavy mortar fire. In addition, CAP H.5 was assaulted by a ground attack with the enemy utilizing grenadiers, B-40 rocket squads and automatic and semi-automatic weapons gaining control of CAP HS and Phu Loc village. In the early morning hours, Company A received approximately 15 B4O rocket rounds along with automatic and semi-automatic weapons fire while set in in its night position. Company B received 45 ... .50 rocket rounds and heavy small arms fire while at Phu Loc District Headquarters on 1 February. Blocking forces from the Battalion Assembly Area. were sent to block enemy movement to the south from Phu Loc with reaction forces moving into Phu Loc to regain CAP H5" All met with stiff resistance from the enemy in the village upon securing CAP H5. The Battalion Assembly area and units in the Phu Loc vicinity received sporadic mortar fire throughout the day. (This information taken from 1/5 Command Chronology for month of February 1968)

A REMBERENCE

I remember Hue in February, 1968. I remember the noble men with whom I both charged across the bitter streets and then sheltered with at end of day after day. I remember the smells, the sights, the thoughts, the expressions on the faces of the injured men I treated. There were so many! I won't go into detail.

I remember the dedication of those valiant Marines. They charged, they fought, and they attacked veraciously. Many were injured but like an unstoppable north bound freight these men pushed forward with magnificent

Battlefield Faith

determination to the bewilderment of the enemy. Wounded men, bandaged men, raggedly attired men, attacked, attacked, attacked! We who are brothers know the powerful spirit and dedication to one another that resides within each of us that pushed us onward. GOD is on the side of the benevolent.

We pushed the villains out. We took the city. We re-established order. We left the world with a memory of our time spent there. We were called "Green Angels" once on another battlefield. The world will never forget the Battle of Hue and the tremendous other battles won by those men who came from a country that places its trust in GOD. We did it for GOD, Country, Corps, and each other. No one could be prouder than this USN corpsman. I was there, in Hue, with the 1st Platoon, Charlie Company, 1st Battalion/5th Marines. They called me "Doc".

I remember one day in February in Phu Bai the word was passed for us to assemble battle ready. The news was that we were soon to be moving out. We would be headed north toward the DMZ to a place called, "Hue City". The North Vietnamese Army had invaded, killed civilian leaders and anyone else that opposed their communist regime and massacred innocents who got in their way. Some Marines were already fighting there and we were to go to reinforce them because our brothers needed some extra support on their flanks. Though it was a large and important city to the South Vietnamese most of us had never heard of the place. Many of us had no idea where it was or what the city and its buildings meant to the locals. Like most of the men I was not in a leadership position to know anything. My greatest concern was how I would take care of "my Marines". I had to be prepared. My "Unit One" Medical bag had to be fully stocked. This bag went everywhere with me. As a Marine has a rifle and many like it and to the individual Marine his rifle is special to him likewise all corpsman in the field carried Unit One Medical Bags. They all looked alike but like the other corpsmen I stocked mine to be my own. I knew what I had in my bag. I knew what I needed and tried to be prepared. As I stated previously, on occasion I had the Marines in our Platoon carry an extra battle dressing in a particular pocket on their uniform. Every man carried it in the same pocket. I knew where to get to that bandage if I needed it. It helped me not to run out in a desperate situation. Hue City was that desperate situation.

Loudermilk

The heroic men that fought in Hue can each give you an eye witness account and probably no two eye witness accounts will be the same. Each story may be similar but also unique. My version comes from my perspective as a "Doc". I was responsible for saving the lives of the wounded men I could in whatever unit I was attached to and I tried with all my being to do just that. We had grown accustomed to fighting in the jungles of Nam. Our experienced men knew what to look for. Once we were patrolling through a village near our outpost. As we slowly moved through the village we noticed a few of the people were acting unusual. We didn't know why. Our squad leader halted us and the men began to move slowly and look for anything out of the ordinary. I remember a small bamboo fence with a gate. We noticed no one was going through the gate. We very carefully moved closer when the point man halted us. I was incredibly impressed at the professionalism of these Marines as we looked around. One of the men sounded off, "Mine!" We instantly stopped in our tracks. It happened that just in front of the bamboo gate a Vietcong had planted a booby trap. I remember witnessing a Marine use a fork to carefully dig into the earth around the mine. He worked patiently as the sweat dripped from his brow. I waited with the rest of the squad and we all remained on alert and aware of our surroundings. After much tedious digging he was successful in uncovering the mine and disarming it. It seemed that the people that we had come here to help had not helped us. This is one memory of the villages and the bush. Hue City was going to be different than the guerilla tactics we were accustomed to in the jungles. We would learn that conventional warfare would be employed in Hue much like the battles that were fought in WWII in the cities of Europe.

 I often think of the events that transpired just before we began our trek to Hue City. The battalion was hastily making all sorts of preparations. We saw trucks heavy laden with supplies facing north and ready to move out at a moment's notice. There were other trucks with drivers at the wheel that were empty for the moment but would be filled to capacity when we got the orders to load up. This was the largest operation I had thus far experienced in my tour of duty here. It seemed like every need that could be addressed was completed including our spiritual. We learned that services for both Protestant and Catholic men had been ordered. A meeting place had been arranged. The Chaplains had made preparations for a time of meditation and when the time came we were given the opportunity to pray. I found that very comforting for I thought, like many of the other men, we were facing the possibility that any one of us could be killed in action and like many of them I sought a peace that can only come through talking to God. Like so many others I took the Lord's advice in the following prayer and prayed:

Matthew 6:9 -13 *After this manner therefore pray ye:*
Our Father which art in heaven, Hallowed be thy name. Thy kingdom come. Thy will be done in earth, as it is in heaven. Give us this day our daily bread. And forgive us our debts, as we forgive our debtors.
And lead us not into temptation, but deliver us from evil: For thine is the kingdom, and the power, and the glory, for ever. Amen. (KJV)

I found comfort in praying the words spoken by our Lord in this passage of scripture and it gave me a sense of calm in the commotion I was seeing all around me. I remember taking communion along with many of the other men that were about to participate in what was to become one of the "bloodiest battles" of the entire Vietnam War.

I felt comfort in spending a while in prayer and needed this personal time to gather my thoughts and pray to GOD as I realized the uncertainty that I was facing. Like the other men I felt the need to make things right between myself and my Maker at such an uncertain time as this. A few moments of prayer gives you time to clear your mind and heart of any baggage you may be carrying. It gives you time to not only pray for yourself but for your buddies and your family at home. I had a lot of questions about what was taking place. Most of us did. However, we were trained not to question those in authority but to have confidence in their leadership and just obey their orders and we were doing just that. I felt it was considerate of them to have included our spiritual welfare as a part of our readiness procedure.

This was the only time I can ever remember us having a prayer service and communion before any battle we were in. We all knew something was up. Storm clouds were appearing on the horizon. We were young. Most of us were teenagers but we all felt we could overcome any challenge the enemy threw at us. We had confidence in our leadership and our training. We loved our country and were proudly representing her here on this foreign field of battle in Southeast Asia as many brave men had done before. We drew strength from one another. There was no one else. We were a brotherhood. We had to face whatever our future had in store for us. The task ahead of us was immense. There were no retreats. We could only forge ahead. We would learn our enemy had been in the city long enough to fortify his positions. He was planted, dug in and had no plans of leaving. We were going to move him out and send him packing back North.

I remember all the commotion of preparation. We assembled in our respective units. I was with Charlie Company, 1st Platoon. I remember the stationing of the 6 bys. These were the big trucks with open beds with sides. A long bench was made on each side in the bed of the trucks and that is where we sat. The top was open. I can recall seeing the twisted remains of many of these trucks on the sides of the roads we traveled that had been victims of land mines. I remember seeing many newsmen with their bags, cameras and gear on this day. We knew they would only be here if we were facing something very important. These were professional news people and we were on the verge of making huge headlines. We weren't told much about what lay ahead of us but we all could sense the feeling of great expectation as we heard the murmuring of our superior officers. Soon after much anticipation we boarded the trucks and when every man was seated the convoy began to roll out of Phu Bai.

During this time of tension and uncertainty and wondering what lay ahead of us I was comforted when I began to think of the words of the Ninety First Psalms:

Psalms 91
He that dwelleth in the secret place of the most High shall abide under the shadow of the Almighty.
I will say of the LORD, He is my refuge and my fortress: my God; in him will I trust.
Surely he shall deliver thee from the snare of the fowler, and from the noisome pestilence.
He shall cover thee with his feathers, and under his wings shalt thou trust: his truth shall be thy shield and buckler.
Thou shalt not be afraid for the terror by night; nor for the arrow that flieth by day;
Nor for the pestilence that walketh in darkness; nor for the destruction that wasteth at noonday.

Battlefield Faith

A thousand shall fall at thy side, and ten thousand at thy right hand; but it shall not come nigh thee.
Only with thine eyes shalt thou behold and see the reward of the wicked.
Because thou hast made the LORD, which is my refuge, even the most High, thy habitation;
There shall no evil befall thee, neither shall any plague come nigh thy dwelling.
For he shall give his angels charge over thee, to keep thee in all thy ways.
They shall bear thee up in their hands, lest thou dash thy foot against a stone.
Thou shalt tread upon the lion and adder: the young lion and the dragon shalt thou trample under feet.
  Because he hath set his love upon me, therefore will I deliver him: I will set him on high, because he hath known my name.
He shall call upon me, and I will answer him: I will be with him in trouble; I will deliver him, and honour him.
With long life will I satisfy him, and shew him my salvation. (KJV)

    This Psalm has been a comfort to many people who have had to face inconceivable challenges in their life. A man or woman can only endure so much alone. Life's load becomes so heavy and we just can't bear it without help. My parents taught us to place our trust in God at an early age although we never attended Church regularly when I was younger. We learned to have faith in God at home. It wasn't until some visitors from a Church of God from our neighborhood called on us one evening and invited us to visit them that we began going regularly. My friends and I used to think there were foreigners attending that church because in those days in the summer months they would leave the windows open for ventilation and you could hear them worshipping in a language that was unknown to us. On one of our visits to the church my Mother and Dad went to the altar and accepted Jesus Christ as their personal Savior. My brothers and sister and I could see an immediate change in them. It wasn't long before our social life was immersed in the activities of the church. We found new friends who seemed to genuinely care about us.
    A seasoned grandfatherly minister by the name of Reverend Huff came one summer to preach a revival. I guess it was the first revival I had ever attended. Each night the air was filled with the joyful sound of the piano and

the echo of people singing praises to the Lord. As a teenager it seemed to me to be an honest and sincere worship from a people who had come to this place of reverence seeking the blessings of the Lord. Most of them had little of life's treasures but had much in the eyes of the Lord. The sincerity of these people and the powerful presence of the Spirit of the Lord made an endearing impression upon me. As the preacher ministered the Word of God I felt compelled to repent of my sins although up until this moment I had not really considered myself a sinner. The Word of God pricked my tender heart so I made my way to the altar with others and I surrendered myself to God's will.

The revival continued as more and more people came to the altar for prayer. I found myself desiring the experience some of the other teenagers had with the Lord. I heard them speak in a language that was strange to me and they exhibited joy and laughter as the Lord blessed them. I decided if there was a deeper experience I wanted it. I went to the altar that night and those who prayed with me said I lingered at the altar for quite some time. I received an experience I have since read about in the book of Acts (2:4) that occurred many years ago on the day of Pentecost. Many people say this event doesn't occur anymore but I can bear witness it happened to me.

Acts 2:4 *And they were all filled with the Holy Ghost, and began to speak with other tongues, as the Spirit gave them utterance.* (KJV)

I feel the Lord empowered me in that revival for the atrocities I would experience in combat in Vietnam. Just before leaving for the Navy I was awakened late one night by what I believe was the Spirit of the Lord. I felt heavily burdened down. I tossed and turned and I could not get back to sleep. I awoke my Mother and she suggested we pray. My mother was a devout Christian who always prayed. Since everyone else was asleep we went to the bathroom, knelt at the bathtub, and began to pray. As we prayed my Mother placed her loving hand upon my back. As we continued to pray we began to feel the awesome power of God and the Holy Spirit praying through us as a peace of God descended and I felt an immediate calm.

Romans 8:26, 27 *Likewise the Spirit also helpeth our infirmities: for we know not what we should pray for as we ought: but the Spirit itself maketh intercession for us with groanings which cannot be uttered. And he that* *searcheth the hearts knoweth what is the mind of the Spirit, because he maketh intercession for the saints according to the will of God.* (KJV)

When our prayer was ended we both had the assurance that whatever my burden was about the Spirit of the Lord had interceded and I could have confidence that everything was taken care of. Two years later I received my combat orders to the Fifth Marines in Vietnam and I was prepared. A person needs a personal life changing experience with the Lord that He can look back on in times of trouble. He needs to be able to say to himself I remember the moment the Lord touched me and reassured me. He needs the confidence he has been in the presence of the Most Holy God! You can feel the presence of God. Christianity is not only teaching, reading and rituals. It is a personal experience with a Holy God.

I felt The Lord assured me that night that He was my Personal Savior. He was not far off but as close as a prayer away. He promised me in His Word that He would never leave me nor forsake me.

Hebrews 13:5 ...*For He Himself has said, "I WILL NEVER LEAVE YOU NOR FORSAKE YOU."* (KJV)

He reminded me that whatever lay ahead of me His grace was sufficient for me.

2Corinthians 12:9 *And He said to me, "My grace is sufficient for you, for My strength is made perfect in weakness..."* (KJV)

That meant that the Lord was on my side. He would support me. He would care for me. To me it meant that the Spirit of The Lord would comfort me whenever fear gripped my soul. The awe-inspiring tranquility I felt that night would be an experience I would draw upon many times in years to come.

The experiences I had with the young people at my church in our worship services gave me an assurance there was someone greater than me or anyone else I could call upon. Those moments with my family and friends provided a foundation of strength to help me to make it through this battle I was facing just ahead. When it seemed the struggle was more than I could bear, I sought the strength of God.

Psalms 27:1 A Psalm of David. *The LORD is my light and my salvation; whom shall I fear? The LORD is the strength of my life; of whom shall I be afraid?* (KJV)

    We began to see a river ahead as our convoy approached the city and its buildings came into view. Shortly after that our convoy came to a stop. We began to dismount the trucks immediately and assembled near the river's edge. It was then that we were instructed to board the flat bottomed Navy boats which were waiting for us and they would carry us across the Perfume River where our assault would begin. As we stood there waiting to board the vessels we beheld an ominous sight. Dark clouds of smoke were rising from the battered city. You could see the destruction that lay ahead. We looked across and to our left as I remember and saw the bridge that had once carried people, animal and machines to and fro lying bent and helpless in the river. The structure had suffered huge devastation and its remains lay crumbled in the water.
    As we boarded our boats the Marines intuitively took their positions on the outer edges of the boat's perimeter and pointed their weapons outward eyeing the area while skillfully looking for the enemy. The boat was already dangerously loaded with ammunition and other supplies but quietly and unceremoniously we just took our positions and began our slow trudge across the water to the other side. The water churned and small waves slapped the sides of the boat as we moved near the middle of the river and closer to the opposite shore. Then without warning we came under enemy attack. We heard the splash of mortar rounds began to fall in the water and explode. The rounds were getting closer as we sailed along. It almost felt like we were part of a movie. Like most young men I had seen many war pictures and saw the actors make their way through the hazards like we were now facing. But this was real. Some men would not be able to get up and walk away from this battle. We had no alternative scenes. We looked ahead. We were trained. We were able. We supported one another. We had each other's back. No enemy would overcome us as we fought together. You can break one stick easier than you can a bunch of sticks tied together. We were a cord bound as one. We had come to free this city from the cruel murderous invaders that held it captive. The trespassers of this city would face the United States Marines.

Battlefield Faith

When we finally got to the other side we could see hundreds of refugees along the river banks. Most of them were cheering as we disembarked. They were grateful we had come to help them. You could see it on their faces and witness it by their actions. They appeared to be a destitute people that had been ravaged by an invading army. We learned later of the horrible atrocities that occurred before our arrival.

Some Marine Units were already fighting in the city when we arrived. It was a literal "war zone". Brick and mortar had been shed from buildings that had been bombarded and the streets were littered with debris. Vehicles were stalled sitting idle along the way as we marched in and we viewed the gruesome sight of the bodies of the helpless, unarmed civilian victims the NVA had slaughtered. We had to adapt quickly. Instead of one or an occasional casualty I would have several at the same time. It's very difficult to put into words the feelings that I would face; the utter desperation, the anguish, the remorse, the helplessness, the loss, the fatigue, the utter indignity of it all. Many of these men would need a highly skilled trauma surgeon and staff and a well-equipped emergency room but they only had me and men like me.

We acquired new skills in Hue. We had grown accustomed to the "bush" but the city was different. If we were entering a building we learned to shout, "Marine coming in!" and when we exited a room or building we shouted, "Marine coming out!" In Hue we had to be aware of the windows. We couldn't walk in front of a window. We had to crawl under the window. If you forgot for a moment you could be the next casualty. One young Marine whom I believe was in Ed Estes' squad, was with us in a rear room. He walked through the house to the front room facing the street to get a better view of the NVA positions. The room had large windows with no curtains and you could see the houses across the street clearly. We didn't know where the enemy was hiding. They had been here for a few weeks ahead of us. They were well embedded in their fighting positions.

Suddenly a shot rang out from the NVA sniper stationed high in one of the buildings on the other side of the street. The Marine fell and alarmingly yelled "corpsman!" I immediately ran to the edge of the doorway which was separating the rooms. Tracer rounds were repeatedly shattering the glass and bouncing around the room like pool balls on a hard break as I crawled closer to where he fell. He kicked the wall with his feet and moved closer to me as I made my way to him. He was hit in the chest but still conscious. I stretched and grabbed him and then pulled him through the doorway that separated the rooms and to the safety of the other room where I lay. I carefully and hurriedly pulled his flak jacket off of him as the sniper continued to rain his projectiles at us. I then had to remove his blood soaked shirt. You never forget the smell of gun powder mixed with blood and sweat. I can hardly walk through some of the sections of a grocery store without remembering this unpleasant smell.

As I carefully examined this brave Marine I could see an entry wound on his chest but when I rolled him over I saw no exit wound. He was covered in blood. I was not able to visually see where the bullet came out. I quickly reacted and started to run my hands over his blood covered chest back forth and found nothing. I then ran my hands under his arm. There it was! The exit wound. I knew then the sniper's round had made its exit. I bandaged him up the best I could and tried my best to reassure him that he would be medevaced quickly and on his way to the Naval Hospital in Danang ASAP.

Together our squad got him out and later word came back to us that the round missed his heart by ¼ of an inch. The bleeding was slowed, he was bandaged, he was comforted, he was reassured and he made it. I did my best to care for him and now he was on his way home. We were all grateful. I thank GOD he made it.

I learned at our reunion in 2017 in Norfolk, Virginia that this was Charlie "Irish" McShane, the Marine that skillfully operated his M60 machine gun and kept the enemy at bay when we were ambushed on that dusty road that night in Hoi An just a few weeks earlier.

Little by little we were advancing against the NVA but Marines were getting wounded one after another. Regardless of our casualties we continued our push ever onward. But like all the other "Docs" I was one corpsman and there were many Marines who needed my help. I didn't have time to think about much except the job at hand. I had to try my best to strive to save as many men as I could. The task was almost unbearable. I was 19 years old. I was not a Trauma Surgeon. I did not have the use of an emergency room. I had no one to help me. I was the only person to stand in the void between life and death for many Marines. I loved them all. We were "brothers" and I had to do my best. I couldn't stop. I didn't have time for a break. When I heard the call, "corpsman" I had to go. I carried at least two canteens because I would need water to soak the bandages when I treated perforated abdominal wounds. A Marine with an empty canteen might need a drink of water. I had to be prepared. I prayed often when fear would engulf me and the dilemma of having to care for tragically wounded men pierced my very being.

1Kings 8:49 *Then hear thou their prayer and their supplication in heaven thy dwelling place, and maintain their cause* (KJV)

    Another Marine was hit in the chest when we were trying to cross one of the streets. With rounds flying back and forth in either direction and the noise of battle thundering in our ears we were dedicated to perform the task that lay ahead of us. It was Marine and corpsman, hand in hand. You've got my back! I've got yours! I ran to answer my call. When I got to him he was reciting his prayers. I asked, "Where are you hit?" He said, "Hail Mary full of grace…" I asked again, "Where are you hit?" He replied, "Hail Mary full of grace…" With rounds screaming over our heads and all around us and bright tracers skimming through the air we both lay there in the rubble that was once part of one of the buildings as I continued my work, and we both prayed.

Isaiah 41:13 *For I the LORD thy God will hold thy right hand, saying unto thee, Fear not; I will help thee.* (KJV)

    As he lay on the ground I began searching for his wounds. I pulled the front of his flak jacket back and opened his blood soaked shirt. I wiped his chest to help me see the wounds more clearly. I noticed a peculiar pattern. I had never seen this before. It looked like the enemy soldier had shot at him from the side. The round appeared to have entered between the spaces of his arm opening on his flak jacket and tumbled across his chest. He had what the cowboys called, "a flesh wound". I tried my best to reassure him. I said, "The round bounced across your chest. It looks like it tumbled end over end." Again he replied, "Hail Mary full of grace…" I cared for his wounds, tagged him and a couple of Marines carried him off as he was praying, "Hail Mary full of grace…" I believe God heard that Marine's prayer.

    I always prayed. I didn't pray long prayers. I didn't have a church with an altar where I could kneel. I prayed as I walked to ambush positions. I prayed on patrol as I kept my eyes open and searched for something unusual like the rest of the squad. I wasn't the only one who trusted God. We all may not pray in the same fashion but God knows our hearts. He sees our sincerity. I've seen men's helmets spin as a round from an enemy AK47 would strike it and hear the man say, "God was with me," as he repositioned it.

We were all young. Many of us were raised in Christian homes. Most of us knew how to say some simple prayer. I learned to talk to God as I would a dear friend and I believe God heard my prayers as well as many of the other men's prayers. I learned I didn't need to learn a well versed passage and ceremoniously recite it for God to hear me. I learned to utter a simple prayer. God became my personal friend with whom I could talk. It's tough to be alone. It's difficult to face unbearable things life throws at you. You can't do it alone. I learned to trust in God. I read of the battles of the Hebrew Children. I read of their faith. I envisioned the great leaders of the Bible standing on mountain tops pouring out their hearts to God interceding for the needs of their people. As I read I felt this was a personal relationship this man had with his God. I learned I could have that too. So I prayed and I found hope in my trust in God.

Because so many men were out of action due to the extreme conditions of this battle some squads were combined and I found myself placed with them in Hue. We learned later on that we had been vastly outnumbered by the invading NVA Army. We were also limited in our resources of how we fought the battle due to something we later learned was "Rules of Engagement" the South Vietnamese government and our higher ups placed on us. It seemed to us that they cared more for their precious buildings than they did for us. Because of this we lost a lot of men and the depleted squads had to be reorganized. As the fierceness of the battle continued I was moved to wherever I was needed. I remember loosing many of our NCOs and having to depend on PFCs as squad leaders. These young men had to accept a great responsibility. They had to mature instantly. They would not only become responsible for themselves but for the men in their squad. I don't remember which Company, Platoon or Squad I was with but we continued fighting together to defeat the enemy and stay alive. I didn't know many of their names and they didn't know mine but I felt like I was numbered with the greatest warriors on the face of the earth. We didn't know how badly we were outnumbered when we were fighting in Hue. We didn't find that out until a few years later when we heard it on the History Channel or news. It didn't matter at the time. We were fighting for one another. Most of us didn't know anything about the politics of war or the governmental controversies in Vietnam. All we knew was to follow orders and do the jobs we were trained to do. And for the moment we were invited here and we were occupying our space and the North Vietnamese Army was intruding. He had to go and we were there to make sure he went. He came in uninvited and had to leave. We would show him the door!

I was a little uneasy sometimes when I would be placed with men who didn't know me and I didn't know them. I guess we watched each other at first. It didn't take long though for any of us to see the dedication and professionalism of one another. I was with one squad once when the units were combined after we had suffered so many casualties. We were coming up on a large building from the rear yard. It was a tall building made of brick. We were moving toward the right rear of it. There was a tree in the next yard whose branches were bending over into the lane just ahead of us that separated the two buildings. We cautiously moved forward until we came to the right rear corner of the building directly ahead of us. Three of us were standing there at an angle. The first man peered around the building and suddenly an enemy soldier launched an RPG round from across the street and hit the brick near the corner and splattered it across the three of us. We were all knocked down by the blast. I had been standing in the middle and the Marines were on either side of me. I was splattered with the brick and dust and my ears were ringing badly but the brick particles had hit the two other men in their faces. Disregarding my own needs I hastily stood up and began treating the wounded men. As I was working some other men came running to our aid.

One young black Marine was hit as he attempted to cross that street ahead of us. He called for help and a white Marine from Alabama that I had talked to briefly hurried to his side. Later we heard the Marine who attempted the rescue was KIA. The other Marine was rescued by his buddies. I remember at Camp Pendleton the Marine Corps Sergeant who was training us told us there was no black and white in the Marine Corps, only Green!

Another corpsman tagged the three of us and moved us to a medevac tent. We were flown by helicopter to Phu Bai to the Battalion Aid Station and seen by the Battalion Surgeon. I believe his name was Dr. Harris and he was from Chicago. He said I had a concussion and he put me on light duty for a couple of days and then I was sent back to Hue.

I remember walking back into the city. It looked like Armageddon had taken place. It resembled the disaster it was. I saw more civilian bodies on the streets as we moved along silently. Dark smoke was rising from the buildings that were still burning. The smell of death permeated the air. We had to stay focused. We couldn't look back. We dare not look ahead. We had to take one step at a time. We could only live for the moment. Each new breath was a blessing. The camaraderie of our fellow Marines was all we had.

We were all Hue City combat veterans now. We knew what lie ahead of us. Our men needed us. We had missed a few days battle. But now we were back. I don't remember any hesitation on anyone's part. I just knew I had been trained to do a job and there were Marines that needed me up ahead. There was a life and death struggle going on but I had to march on and take my place with them. No one spoke a word as we moved forward. I whispered a prayer as we moved along to confront the battle each of us would face just ahead. I prayed for God to be with us and give us peace as the dust from the street of that city battlefield rose up in tiny clouds with each step we took. We needed God to bless us. We needed God to be gracious to us. We needed God to grant us peace. With snipers rounds bouncing all around us and the noise of war echoing through the air we reached deep into our resolve and sought courage to march onward.

Joshua 1:9 *Have not I commanded thee? Be strong and of a good courage; be not afraid, neither be thou dismayed: for the LORD thy God is with thee whithersoever thou goest.* (KJV)

2Chronicles 20:15 *..., Thus saith the LORD unto you, Be not afraid nor dismayed by reason of this great multitude; for the battle is not yours, but God's.* (KJV)

This looks like one of the places where we may have sought shelter for the night. I think that's me in the back looking out.

Chapter 11

A Man's Groan, A Baby's Cry

The enemy deployed his forces in fighting holes and trenches in depth in well built up areas along back streets and intersections with interlocking fires. Bomb shelters were constructed in houses to their rear to afford them adequate cover and concealment from air attacks. Interrogation of Private Nguyen Quand Kham of the 11th Company, 416th Battalion revealed that his company was not prepared for general withdrawal from the Citadel. After first contact with U.S. forces, subject's company on order commenced a series of holding engagements which were designed to make this battalion's advance as costly as possible pending the dispatch of fresh enemy reinforcements from outside the city. (of Hue)

The enemy fought a repeated delaying action using B-49 rocket launchers, grenades, automatic and semi-automatic weapons with 82mm and 60mm mortars in support. During withdrawals, snipers and B-40 rocket teams as well as grenadiers were left interspersed in the area to kill and harass friendly troops as they pressed enemy withdrawal.

(This information taken from 1/5 Command Chronology from report of month of April 1968)

I remember my friend, Charles Morgan. He was another brave Marine. He was in Corporal Ed Estes's squad. Eddie was as fine a Texas bred leader of men as one could be. I was with them on this fateful day. We moved into our position along "Phase Line Green" our Platoon and others of our company had established. The enemy was entrenched just a few feet away from us across the street. We learned later that they were not only in the buildings but they were dug in and fortified between them as well. I was kneeling there with Charles between two buildings on our side of the street looking across toward our enemy. There was an old wooden fence in front of us and it had some old wire on it helping to hold it together. The NVA were hailing rounds at us feverously. They were hitting all around us and bouncing off of everything in their path. They were trying their best to discourage us to put it lightly. Charles replied with his M16 then turned to me and said, "I believe my sights are off, Doc. I think I bumped them on something moving in here." "I guess I'll have to use Kentucky Windage." I nodded agreeably at him. Then he reloaded and continued firing.

At one point we had our orders to try and cross the street. I can't remember the circumstances but my friend Charles was one of the Marines who tried. He gathered himself and focused his attention on the direction he would take. I don't remember anyone saying anything. He took off quickly and went down after moving toward the middle of the street as the NVA sniper's round hit its target. He fell not far from the rest of us. We knew someone had to go help. I knew I would go if that is what our squad leader ordered. I prepared myself. All of the other men were also making ready. We were all becoming uneasy. A difficult decision had to be made immediately.

Ed made it! He was our leader and all of us respected him greatly. I remember my friend Eddie well. I recall once we were out on a Platoon size patrol. We were all walking down a path through the jungle. Ed had the point. Suddenly he gave the signal for the platoon to stop. We all halted and waited. Ed saw smoke in the distance, in the middle of the jungle that many men would not have seen. He saw the sunlight glimmer across a small strand of fishing line or wire stretched across the path and knew the enemy had probably prepared an ambush along the booby trapped trail. His experience, his unique oneness with his surroundings and his attention to detail saved not only his life but the lives of the men following him.

Here we were facing another dilemma. Ed knew something had to be done about one of his men that had gone down. He wasn't going to leave a Marine alone. Each of us would do whatever he asked of us. As we were trying to figure out the best thing to do Ed walked over to where some of us had gathered in that large house, turned to us with a determined look upon his face and said, "I wouldn't send any of my men out to do something I wouldn't do myself." With that he readied his M16 and bolted out of the front door before anyone could say anything. We heard some shots ring out and immediately Eddie ran back through the door. He ran to me, looked me in the face and fell at my feet. I dropped everything. I hastily knelt down beside him and quickly looked for his wound. I began earnestly to try and save my friend's life. We had gone on ambush and patrols together. We had talked about home and our loved ones back in the States often. He told me he was married. I accompanied him to Danang once where he bought an anniversary present for his wife in Texas. There are good men. Eddie was a great man. Now he needed me. I would do all I could do to save him.

But sometimes no matter how hard we try or how badly we want things to happen some situations are just out of one's control. I just couldn't give up. He was my friend. I had come to love him and Charles and the other Marines with whom I served like brothers. As hard as I tried and as much as I wanted I couldn't help either of them. I had never felt the incredible weight of defeat as I felt at that moment. Two of the best men we had were gone. A squad leader had disregarded his own safety to save one of his men. Ed Estes had pushed aside his own feelings and what may happen to him to save his friend. Ed was a Texan. Charles was from Louisiana. They were from neighboring states. They had become brothers in arms. They were two of the best our country had to offer. I'll never forget them. As long as we remember them they live!

John 15:13 *Greater love hath no man than this, that a man lay down his life for his friends.* (KJV)

There is no time in war to pause for grief. You can't release your emotions. You have to control yourself. You have to bottle up your anguish. There is no time for tears of sorrow. There are no long farewells. You live and die together. The ones who survive take care of those who can no longer do it for themselves. A man is full of life one day. You have your morning chow together. You talk some when the day is new. You try to plan for the struggles the day may bring. Hand in hand you face the mountains of despair together with your other friends and men you have learned to call brother. But now you must leave your friend and move on. You won't see him in this life again. Your memories are all you have. These memories are not of parties, going to the lake or picnics. They are not of laughing and

Battlefield Faith

gatherings with family and friends. They are of war and of men fighting to stay alive. They are memories of sharing what little food you have and drinking from the same canteen. They are memories of traversing rivers and streams and watching out for one another. God bless these valiant men.

Very close to the time Ed and Charles went down a round from an enemy sniper's rifle hit our Platoon Sergeant, John "Mother" Mullan, in the side of the head. He collapsed on the ancient soil of Hue. He was performing his job of leading Marines when he fell. I had so many horrendous episodes occurring simultaneously that I don't remember the exact critical move we made there. His first battle dressing was applied to slow down the horrendous amount of blood he was losing. He was prepared for medical evacuation. I was taking care of so many casualties. I tended to them as best I could. The men watched over John as he lay silent on that war torn street waiting to be medevaced.

After checking John over I began to walk away with the squad I was with and then I had a feeling to turn and look back toward him. I saw a young Marine near him and it appeared he was going to remove his bandage because it was blood soaked and replace it with a clean one. I screamed, "Stop!" And he did. If he would have removed that dressing "Mother" may not have made it. I hurried back to him and quickly placed a clean battle dressing over the blood soaked one and gave instructions it was to stay that way as he was medevaced.

We had to keep moving. We couldn't let our guard down. The NVA were just across the street. They thought they were an unmovable force but they were about to face an unstoppable action: The United States Marines!

Being a corpsman I was a continual observer. My job was to save lives. There were times when I carried an additional weapon other than my 45 but here I had no time for anything else. I had to do everything in my limited power to save the wounded Marines destiny had placed in my path.

As the fighting continued we were running low on water and had to find some somewhere. As we searched we found large Roman like urns in some of the houses and looked inside them. It appeared to be a water source the people used in their homes. We had no choice but to fill our canteens with it. Without hesitation most of us added the usual large dose of halazone tablets to the water before drinking it. Although the halazone caused the water to taste like bleach we used it to protect ourselves from dysentery and other bacteria that the water might contain. I also remember the ominous task of how we divided up the c-rations of the men who had been medevaced. We were young but we were warriors. We had been trained by our country and sent to a far-away land to fight for a reason most of us did not understand. But we learned we must do our best to survive! And that is what we did.

In some of the houses we found large, opened 100 pound sacks of rice which had labels which read, "Donated by the People of the United States of America". Undoubtedly the NVA had been eating this food supplied by our nation to sustain them while they fought us! I don't know to whom the rice was given originally but it had fallen into enemy hands. On one occasion a family offered to share with us what little food they had and we in turn shared what we had with them.

I recall that on the way in we had passed a store with its owner still inside. The city was almost deserted. We couldn't figure why he was still there. We asked him to share some of his drinks of whatever he had in them. He was reluctant to offer us any. Even though we had come to save his city he didn't want to share anything with us. It's ironic because the next time we passed his store it had been hit with explosives and looked like it had been ransacked. We found a few items of interest and helped ourselves. We put some of our Tang that a few of us had into the bottled carbonated water we found. Then we continued on. It would soon be dark and we had to find shelter somewhere in the ruins for the night. We all had to make sure we all knew one another's whereabouts.

The Baby

I was with my Platoon Commander, Lieutenant Nick Warr, radioman Eugene "Benny" Benware and a few more Marines on this eventful evening. We had survived another day in the Battle for Hue City. We were gaining ground but at a very great expense. We continued to lose men either by being wounded or killed in action. The choppers were very busy. Leisure time was not something we even thought of nor had time for. Nick and our group found a hooch where we could spend the night. The family that lived there hadn't left. They opened their home to us. They were very friendly. They were thankful we had come to rid their city of the vermin that had infested it and killed many of their beloved citizens among whom were school teachers and leaders of their community we later learned.

The man of the house brought out some choice items he had undoubtedly been saving for a special occasion for his family. He shared some cookies and I remember a can of "leeks". I had never of heard of leeks. I didn't bother with them but I did have a cookie. The Marines shared some of whatever they had. We felt welcome in their home and settled in for the night. They treated us very well. I think they felt safer with us staying with them.

    Then sometime during the night a runner came to inform us that a Vietnamese woman was about to have a baby and needed help. Nick turned to me and said I needed to go and see what I could do. The Marines led me to the temporary home where the woman was with her husband. Two other corpsman were arriving that I knew and we were all glad to see each other. Ken and Terry were their names. I have forgotten their last names. They were exceptional corpsman.

    I spoke a little High School French and began to talk with the husband. We understood each other somewhat. After talking with him we began to reassure his wife. You could see she knew we were there to help and she appeared to relax a little. We got there just in time. She began to go into labor shortly after we all had settled in and each of us tried to remember our lessons from Hospital Corps School, Great Lakes and Field Medical School, Camp Pendleton. Up to this point we had been facing tragic scenes of death and destruction. Now everything had changed! We were going to be the first ones to welcome a new life into the world. We were very excited. We all made our preparations and when it was time the Mother had no problems giving birth. This was her third child I believe she told us. The baby arrived and it was a beautiful little girl with a full head of black hair. When he heard the baby's cry the Father came near and asked, "Garson?" I said, "Non, c'est une petite fille!" A smile arose on his face and you could see he was well pleased. We finished our work and wrapped the baby in the cleanest blankets we could find. The owners of the house had long left and the house was large and accommodating.

    We let the Mother hold her new daughter for a while and then she felt she needed to sleep and she showed her trust in us when she asked us to care for the baby while she rested. We carried the infant to a larger front room where there was a big bed with mattress and blankets. The head of the bed sat against the wall to the left when you entered the room from the back of the house. Then we gently placed the newborn on the bed and pulled the covers up on her. She began to rest peacefully.

    Due to so many casualties our platoon didn't have enough men to supply security for us that night so they gave each of us corpsman an M16. We took our posts. We decided one man needed to be at the rear door and two at each of the large windows in the front room. I was in the front room on the left side facing the street and one of the other corpsman was on the right. The large handcrafted wooden bed held the sleeping infant directly behind us.

As the night lingered on everything became still. We all knew there would be no sleep for us this night. We dozed and watched each other and rotated our positions but we never slept. After we were at our posts for a while maintaining our vigilance and looking for the smallest sign of the enemy our senses were heightened. I think we had been in Hue for a few days and had endured the ominous fatigue of battle. We knew our Marines were on each side of us in the other buildings but we didn't know their exact positions. The ticking of time was heard by all from somewhere in the house. It sounded like an old clock that had been ticking for quite a while. Then suddenly the stillness of the night was broken by a "bong" "bong" "bong" directly behind us. Instinctively and without hesitation the two of us at the windows whipped around and pointed our weapons only to see a very large antique looking clock on the mantle above the bed sounding off where the baby slept. The noise had not disturbed her at all but it sure made the hair stand up on the back of our necks and sent a chill down our spines!

I often think of this little girl and how her life might have been. I think of how she had to grow up in a Communist society. I think of what she may have become. I pray she has had a good life. I hope her parents told her of how she came into this world and who it was that came to liberate her city. She was born that dark night in February 1968 during the heat of the Battle of Hue City and now she was surrounded by Marines all around. The enemy was just across the narrow street in the houses directly facing the building where we stood our watch and where the baby lay but the child slept peacefully.

Sometimes we question why we have been placed in a certain position but that Mother, Father, and baby needed us. War had taught us to hate the enemy. We hated him for what he did to us. We hated him for what he did to the innocents of Hue City. We hated him for the War we were so deeply involved in. But as deep as our hate was we found love for this innocent baby we had helped bring into the world. I read where the Jews were hated and despised and put into slavery. Their babies were slaughtered but the mother of Moses placed her baby in a little ark and the hand of God caused the daughter of Pharaoh to find him. Though many of her people hated the Jews she found love for the infant in her heart.

Exodus 2:10 *And the child grew, and she brought him unto Pharaoh's daughter, and he became her son. And she called his name Moses: and she said, Because I drew him out of the water.*

The next morning we gathered our belongings and bid farewell to the family and rejoined our men. Nick asked how things went and I related our story to him. I think he was a little proud too.

I can't remember the order of events but Nick was needed somewhere and I was needed somewhere else. As we were passing a mortar crew they yelled for some help. They said some Marines were about to be overrun and called for assistance. They told me to start opening some packages of rounds and I did as I was told. After a while they got a call for cease fire and we moved on.

Here's Mike again and part of a mortar crew this time. He's holding two mortar rounds.

Lt. Nick Warr assembled what was left of his platoon for a rescue party. A squad had been searching for NVA soldiers and advancing toward their position crossing through the rabble of fallen buildings. At one point they had to take cover quickly and move through a building situated in their path. It appeared they had started taking incoming fire and they all dove into the nearest room as they ran down the hallway of this building. Some NVA soldiers circled around and threw grenades through a window in the room the men had dived into.

All of the men received some kind of injury, some life threatening. As we took our places in the back of the building Nick told me to run through the open door and down the hallway then dive into the room and see if I could help these Marines as he and his men would provide cover fire for me. I looked at the house, marked where I thought the men would be down the dark hallway. I noticed the door on our end of the house was being slung back and for by the wind. As I looked through the hallway from where we were finding our places I saw the door on the opposite end of the hallway was doing the same.

Nick timed the event perfectly. The Marines began to open fire. As they did I quickly began my run as fast as I could go while enemy tracer rounds screamed through the hallway past me as the NVA was trying to put me down. By God's grace I made it to the room which was on my left and dove into it and hit the deck. The men were all lying on the wooden floor, some groaning. I realized I had a huge task ahead of me trying my best to administer aid to each of the men's wounds while trying to keep each one of them alive.

Our buddies outside did their job well and soon the area was secure. We began to carry the men to the rear of the building, our starting point. The Marines then began the task of carrying the casualties to a pickup station where they would be transported by "mule" to the LZ (landing zone) for more intense treatment. This was all done quickly and efficiently.

Time for Church

We were still engaging the enemy at every turn but when a Sunday came a Chaplain made his way out to us. A suitable hooch was found by the Chaplain's crew. They had cleaned it up some to resemble a church. Those of us that wanted to assembled in the little building and after we were settled the service began. The Chaplain gave an inspirational message. I was thankful that he had come by. I needed to get a prayer through as well as all of the men who had gathered there. We crowded into that hooch and the Chaplain spoke some uplifting and supportive words. Our Chaplains, both

Battlefield Faith

Protestant and Catholic, were dedicated men. They volunteered for some hazardous duty to bring The Word of GOD to us on the battlefield.

I remember Tex. He was a big man. I am six foot tall and he was bigger than me. He was somewhat soft spoken and he was going to complete his task in Nam and go to Nashville and pursue a career in music. He was a songwriter and singer. Tex had a brother that had preceded him to Nam as a Marine. He was tragically KIA and Tex mourned his death. Tex told me once that he would go to the cemetery and lie down on the grass next to his brother's grave as he was growing up and promised him he would one day become a Marine and avenge him.

The men I was with this day approached a very wide and open courtyard. The buildings surrounding it seemed to be in a semi-circle. Across on the other side we saw a large tree in full bloom with large limbs. We saw no enemy soldiers so we began to move. The Marines across from us started to move also. Tex must have been designated to make his way across first as we saw him began to jot across the courtyard and under the tree. As he reached the tree a sniper from one of the buildings fired his weapon and Tex went down. He was quite a ways off from us but we recognized his stature. He was an unmistakably big man.

A news reporter that had ridden to Hue with us in one of the trucks wanted me to run across the open field that was under fire from snipers located in the high positions of the tall buildings that surrounded the area and see if I could save him. I don't know who Tex was with but I am sure his men reacted in the way they had been trained. A few more casualties would have made a great story for that reporter. I stayed with my squad this time and felt the other corpsman that was with Tex would take care of the situation.

We did move toward Tex's position later and no one could have saved him. He was KIA instantly. We all felt great remorse losing him that way. He had told me once that he had joined the Marine Corps and had come to Nam to kill one "gook" for his brother. Tex killed his "gook" but then he was also killed. He will always be remembered by his friends. He told us he had written many songs and had made a tape to be aired when he got home. So many talented young men were lost in that battle.

There were so many casualties and when evening came we settled in to our post for the night. It was at this time that many thoughts went through my mind. My uniform was torn, my face was dirty, and my hands had dried blood upon them. The stench of death pervaded the atmosphere. I had taken care of so many casualties and seen more than any teenager should ever have to see. Often I would ask myself, "What would I do if I had to choose between losing my arms and hands or my feet and legs?" Which would I choose? I thought, "Well, I like to play the guitar and I like to drive. I figured if I lost my arms and hands I could do neither. On the other hand if I lost my feet and legs I could do both. I would have no trouble playing the guitar and I could have my car rigged up to accommodate me. These are some of the awful thoughts that permeated my mind in that war. I imagine other men were battling the same thoughts. Many men lost their extremities. I pray for them that God will make their burdens light.

Chapter 12

Heavy Hands and Heart

All told, 142 Marines were killed in action during Operation HUE CITY, and nearly 1,000 were badly wounded and med-evaced. Several thousand NVA and Viet Cong soldiers lost their lives during their failed Tet Offensive, and an estimated 5,000 Vietnamese civilians, most of them considered leaders of the South Vietnamese people, had been rounded up and murdered by the invaders. Although the results of this battle were initially badly misreported, and the leaders of the American government were severely and negatively affected by this, the actual results of this historic battle showed that the Viet Cong were eliminated as a fighting force, and the NVA were not able to mount any military offensive of any significance until four years later.
(This information taken from http://1-5vietnamveterans.org/15-combat-ops/)

Like the other men who had fought in this long and arduous "Battle of Hue City" I had grown weary. My hands were heavy and the burden of my heart was almost too much to bear! I remember the story of Moses as he led the Children of Israel in battle. Israel was victorious as long as Moses raised his hands but he became weary and needed a little help.

Exodus 17:12 *But Moses' hands were heavy; and they took a stone, and put it under him, and he sat thereon; and Aaron and Hur stayed up his hands, the one on the one side, and the other on the other side; and his hands were steady until the going down of the sun.* (KJV)

26 February 1968
Monday

Dear Mother, Dad & Family,

Well, I thought I would drop you all a few lines to let you know everything is going fine & the Lord is helping me every hour.

I am writing this letter in Hue City. We are staying in their University overnight. It's a real big school & modern. We are across the river from where we were fighting.

I wrote you all a letter this morning but I thought I'd write again because I might be busy

II

some other time.

Most of us don't know where we are going tomorrow but we think there is another operation. I know whatever it is God will be with me.

I sure will be glad when I get home so I can go to our church. I sure do miss that.

> Well, I'll close for now but will write write again soon.
>
> Love,
> John
>
> P.S. Tell everyone to write & I'll try my best to answer their letters.

Often life throws obstacles in our path. Like many other people I try to tackle them myself most of the time. All too often you come to a roadblock life has put in your way. Sometimes it is a problem that seems a little bit more than you can handle. But what do you do? Where do you go? Where do you get a helping hand? Again, if you are like me and quite a lot of other people you don't know the answers to these questions. It was difficult for me to seek help and it took some time for me to trust anyone or believe anyone would understand my dilemma. A friend at work who was also a combat veteran said to me one day, "John, I think you have the same problem that I do." I said to him, "What problem?" He began to talk to me about being a combat veteran and he said he had come to the end of his rope. When he realized his problem was too big for him to handle he did the only thing he could. He took his DD214 and went to the emergency room at his local VA Hospital. He was directed to a Medical Social Worker who guided him to the right people. He told me he waited as long as he could without asking for help but he said it was the best thing he had ever done for himself. So I would say to you my combat brother or sister, "Don't wait. Go now. Seek help. It is an honorable thing you have done for your country, now your country will help you heal. Healing is a process. You must initiate it. Please believe me. I am speaking from experience. I know how you feel. There are many like us. Do your family a favor now while you can. God Bless you.

Psalms 62:8 *Trust in him at all times; ye people, pour out your heart before him: God is a refuge for us.* (KJV)

2Corinthians 1:3, 4 *Blessed be God, even the Father of our Lord Jesus Christ, the Father of mercies, and the God of all comfort; Who comforteth us in all our tribulation, that we may be able to comfort them which are in any trouble, by the comfort wherewith we ourselves are comforted of God.* (KJV)

We lived day by day and night by night. We turned off much of our feelings until we were practically emotionally numb. I had a VA counselor tell me one time that in life you have many switches. You learn to turn them on and off as you need them. She said that in wartime you have two switches. A man must learn the art of survival. I was so full of frustration and anxiety that I felt emotionally drained. I didn't feel like I could take anymore but I knew I would have to if that was how it had to be. I knew I needed to be relieved. My six months of field duty with 1st Platoon, Charlie Company was coming to a close and I was to enter the next phase of my tour with the 1st Marine Division. The NVA had been defeated in Hue. The cleanup would soon begin. My platoon and company would be moving to a new area and continue the fight against the communist aggressors in another part of Vietnam.

Dear Mother, Dad, & Family,

I praise God that I am able to write you all today. The reason I haven't for so long is that we've been in the field & on an operation at Hue City. There were a lot of U.S. casualties & I praise the Lord that I wasn't one of them. He is surely keeping his almighty hand upon me.

I want you all to pray that I will get stationed in BtS or the Medical Battalion. I know God will have his will & that's what is important.

We have been fighting

in about the same way as they did in WW II when they took France. It has really been rough.

I am feeling pretty good & I'm in pretty good health.

Are you having any revivals there or have you already had one? Let me know what's happening in the Church. How is our pastor? He sent me a Christmas card.

Well, pray for me & I'll write again soon.

Love,
John

This is where many of us stayed for a night when I wrote the letter. We had pushed the invading North Vietnamese Army out and were in the process of giving the city back to the people who lived there.

During the first week of March in 1968 a new corpsman showed up and said he was my replacement. I was very surprised. I welcomed him and asked him what his name was and I told him I would never forget it. He answered and said, "My name is Ben Hurd!" I thought, "Wow!" I know I'll never forget that name. It reminded of the Ben Hur movie with Charleston Heston. I prayed Ben would do well and I felt remorse when I left my brothers in Charlie Company.

February 1968

Dear Mother, Dad & Family,

    I take this time to try and catch up on some letters that I have received.

    The operation we were on is finally over, (Operation Hue City), & I praise God I came out O.K.

> The news is now that our company is going to the rear in Phu Bai to regroup. We had 13 men left out of 54 in the 1st Platoon. There were quite a few casualties but the Lord brought me through on top & I praise him for it.
>
> Well, pray for me & I'll write again soon. Love, John

    As my letter states, we had 13 men left out of 54 in our 1st Platoon who fought in Operation Hue City with us. Some of them were KIA and some of them were WIA. I was there for many of them. There was another corpsman in our platoon there also. We never worked together much because that was our routine. We had to work separately to cover our squads. But the battle was over. The victory had been won. We were highly outnumbered but by the grace of God we overcame them and they fled back north toward Hanoi.

Psalms 44:5 *Through thee will we push down our enemies: through thy name will we tread them under that rise up against us.* (KJV)

Psalms 18:37, 38, 39 *I have pursued mine enemies, and overtaken them: neither did I turn again till they were consumed. I have wounded them that they were not able to rise: they are fallen under my feet. For thou hast* *girded me with strength unto the battle: thou hast subdued under me those that rose up against me.* (KJV)

The calm after the storm, that's me in the middle with some grateful kids. They surely knew how to hide when the battle was raging.

The Battle of Hue City was finally over. We praise our God for being with us and giving us strength to defeat the invading enemy. Now the people of Hue can clean up, heal and hopefully live in peace and harmony.

My first assignment after leaving Charlie Company was with 81 Mortars. All I remember about their location is that they were dug in and had their weapons set up alongside a mountain near a main road that led to the top of the peak.

3 March 1968

Dear Mother, Dad & Family,

I thought I'd write again to let you know everything is going fine & God is blessing me. He is really answering my prayers. Last month I asked God to send some replacements to our company so to relieve us and this month I was relieved.

I'm with 81 mortars now. The army calls it light artillery.

We have a new chaplain. His name is Jack Phillips and he's from Minnesota. He preached on the 23rd psalms last Sunday. He's a pretty good talker.

We're not outside in the rain much. I stay with the C.P. (Command Post) group. This is where the orders are given. We are living in an abandoned house. The people fled to safety south of here. Practically the whole town is deserted. They're feeding us two meals a day but I manage to get a little extra here & there. We get plenty to eat back at our base though.

There was a Lam (land to air missile) site on top of the mountain and a battalion aid station also. When I was with Charlie Company we didn't have

Battlefield Faith

much of a chance to get away for some time of our own. It seemed like we worked most of the time. As I previously stated, we had early mine sweeps, daily patrols, nightly ambushes, convoy duty and other things. Our job was demanding. But when I got to 81s I did get a chance to get away.

5 March 1968

Dear Mother, Dad & Family,

Well, I thought I would write you all a few lines to let you know everything is going fine & the Lord is really helping me.

We are in a pretty well secured area now and will be here for approximately 3-4 weeks.

Tomorrow my buddie & I are going to try & go to Da Nang for the day. Mainly for recreation, but we're going to pick up some supplies.

I guess I'm going to pick up E-5 this month

or next. I hope its this month.

We ae undergoing training more but it's mostly for the line companies. I'm still in 81 Mortars. Praise God.

I'm still expecting your package.

Well, pray for me & I'll write again soon.

Love,
John

P.S. Write Soon

February was coming to an end and March was beginning to appear and we welcomed it. My birthday was in March. I turned 20 years old in I Corps in 1968. I didn't get a cake that year but I have made up for it since. My wife, Sandy, always makes sure it happens.

There were no lines in Nam. Each unit had to secure their own area. That's why I wrote in my letter that we were in a pretty secure place. In the Navy you have to take a test and pass some practical factors to get promoted. I couldn't do that in combat so I got a field promotion to E5. I was to become an HM2. That's a second class petty officer corpsman. I felt pretty satisfied with myself. I was 20 years old and now I would become an E5.

With all of my time with Charlie I don't remember ever getting sick where it hindered my work. We moved around all of the time and I guess that was good for us in some ways. Here with the 81s I never moved around. We stayed where we were dug in. I feel the result of my stationary assignment here led to my getting a chest cold which turned into a case of bronchitis. I thought I needed to see a Doctor and get some antibiotics. I told the Senior NCO I needed to get some medical care and he gave me the ok to leave.

I had to find my own way the closest Aid Station which was at the top of the mountain so I walked out to the road to hitch a ride. I guess a few vehicles passed without stopping but a man riding a small motorbike did offer me a lift. I told him I would give him a box of c-rations for a ride. He gladly accepted the offer. The bike began to struggle as we neared the half way mark and the man stopped the bike and wanted me to get off. I was sick. I was tired. I had no intention of walking the rest of the way. He continued to demand I get off. I thought to myself this guy might have buddies waiting out here in the bush somewhere so I have to get serious. I pulled out my 45, pointed it in his direction and said, "De di Mau", which meant at this point, "Get the bike going or this could be your last ride! He got the message and the bike found new power. I wouldn't have shot him but he didn't know that.

We continued up the mountain road and finally reached the top. I handed the man a box of Ham and Lima Beans. He screamed, "No, No! No! Number 10,000! All I could do was wheeze and laugh as I handed him the C- rats. I could hardly believe he knew what they were. I guess I was not the first American he offered a ride to.

Battlefield Faith

I was a little uneasy as I continued my trek to the Aid Station. All I was carrying at this point was my 45 but I had it locked and loaded. As I continued walking I smelled the odors of a Mama San preparing a meal for her family and I heard vehicles in the distance straining to get up the other side of the mountain. I was always alert. I didn't want to fall prey to an unsuspecting enemy hiding in the bush as I walked. I wheezed and sweated as I finally made it to my destination and then up the wooden steps of sickbay and I was safe.

As fate would have it I recognized the corpsman in charge. I had served with him at the Naval Hospital in the Philippines. He was a friendly guy and he had already made HM2 (E5, which is equivalent to Sergeant in the Marine Corps). We talked a while. He guessed why I came since I was wheezing so badly. Like a good Doc he treated my illness and placed me on light duty. We continued to reminisce as I began to catch my breath again.

I recovered from the bronchitis in a few days and the Battalion Aid Station had me reassigned to them temporarily since they were short-handed. That was fine with me. It got me some healthier duty and I would have a dry place to sleep and some hot chow every day.

I 7 March 1968
   Thursday

Dear Mother, Dad & Family,

I thought I would drop you all a few lines to let you know everything is going fine.

I am now staying with the B.A.S. since it is so close to 81½. We are sitting on a mountaintop, 12 miles north of DaNang. The place is called 1st LAAM @ HAI VAN pass. I praise God for helping me and for protecting me.

I'm studying up on my medicine now and learning a little bit more.

II

I got a chance to go to Da Nang yesterday. Boy, did I really eat! My friend & I both had a ravioli dinner & also a chicken dinner at once. It sure was good. We're getting hot chow now, though. It's pretty good too.

I actually have it made here. ~~[scratched out]~~ We get up at 0600 and the man at the chow hall brings some pastries down, we have our own coffee pot, and we eat breakfast. At 0730 we hold sick call for the battalion, or whichever companies are here. After

III

that we straighten things up and the good part of the day is our own. We hold sick call again at 1330 (1:30 PM). Most of what we are doing now is get straightened out since we have only been here 2 days.

How is everyone around home? If you see Buss & Larry tell them to write me.

Well, I want you all to pray for me & I'll write again soon.

Love,
John

Promotion

I wasn't able to take a customary exam for advancement but I got a field promotion to HM2 (E5) and then I was reassigned to the Regimental Aid Station to finish out my tour. This was a permanent assignment and I would continue getting a daily ration of hot food and a dry place to sleep. Wow again!

18 March 1968

Dear Mother, Dad & Family,

Well, praise the Lord for answering another prayer. Here I sit in B.A.S. and I'm getting transferred from here to R.A.S. (Regimental Aid Station) in Phu Bai for the rest of my tour I guess. I sure do praise God for helping me. I know He is with me.

It's pretty warm today and know its going to get warmer. I guess that's better than rain all the time though.

Battlefield Faith

I missed Charlie Company and went by their tent whenever I could. I was able to occasionally get a case of cold Cokes from the General's supplies in Phu Bai because I knew a guy! I would take it over to my Marines and they were glad to get it. I kept a case every once in a while and took it to the RAS (Regimental Aid Station).

I no longer had to sleep on the ground. I got more rest. I had more personal time. I had hot chow every day and a rack in our sick bay hooch to sleep in. The hooch had a tin roof and plywood floors. The plywood came up about four feet from the floors on the sides and wire screen continued up the wall from there to the ceiling. This construction allowed the air to circulate. I had a more comfortable position but I still had to be available for any extra duties that would come up.

I even had some leisure time which I had not had for quite a while. I was able to go on R & R in Japan where I bought some things and one of them was a guitar. I have played off and on since I was a teenager. I never really got very good up to this point. I just enjoyed getting away to myself and strumming a few chords. It gave me great enjoyment and it was good therapy in that it tended to calm my nerves when I strummed.

7 April 1968
(Sunday)

Dear Mother, Dad & Family,

Well, things are going pretty good and there are not too many patients coming in so I thought I'd write a few lines to let you know the circumstances.

I live inside now at the Regimental Aid Station. We have wooden floors & a tin roof. I'm writing at the sick call desk at present.

It is sunny & warm out today and I praise God that I can enjoy the weather instead of "humping the hills".

As things are in order for me to accept my promotion for E-5 I might have to extend 94 days. My chief is from Cincinnati (Hyde Park). He said it would be worth it. He said I'd get a better job & I know more money. I want you all to pray concerning this. I don't really know if I should or not.

Oh, yes, I'm sending some movie film of Japan home. Be sure and have this developed. I will buy a projector when I come home.

Well, pray for me and I'll write again soon.   Love, John

Battlefield Faith

March had come and gone and April was here. I was glad to see each month pass for it brought me closer to the time I would be going home. You really don't know how much you appreciate your homeland until you leave it. "Dorothy" was right in the Wizard of Oz movie when she said, "There's No Place Like Home". If I was home I'd be thinking about fishing and picnics and those warm summer days. I'd be thinking about hearing the children in the parks playing and their joyful voices echoing through the air. But I had some duty to perform before I would be able to enjoy those times again. I had completed my required six months with my infantry company and had settled in to my new surroundings. Adjusting to it was a little odd for me at first. I went from mud to clean and being hot and wet and sometimes miserable to comfortable, clean and dry. I was the only medical person when I was with my squads but I would be assisting a Doctor here and I couldn't have been placed with anyone any better than Doctor Brock. He was a fine southern gentleman and a very dedicated doctor.

I remember I was ordered to fly out to a village once and hold sick call. I couldn't tell you where but when we flew in there was a huge number of people seeking medical care. We set up immediately and started seeing those waiting in line. We didn't have a Doctor going out with us. I remember a Marine Corps Officer being in charge. I was a little hesitant going out to the bush again after being in what some of us called "the rear" but those feelings left me when I saw the little children, toddlers and babies and looked into the eyes of the Mothers holding them in their arms. They were the innocent victims of this cruel communist incited war.

20 April 1968
Saturday

Dear Mother, Dad & Family,

I was really glad to get your letter today and know everything is going fine.

> I am having to go out tomorrow with our forward Regimental Command Post. They are staying in tents. I only have to stay there 10 days and then someone will relieve me. Then I come back to Phu Bai. The Lord is with me & I try and read my Bible every day. I'm also practicing on the guitar I bought in Japan.
>
> I will mail you the things I bought this coming payday.
>
> Well pray for me & remember me at Church & I'll write again soon.
>
> Love,
> John

    There was a Vietnamese man there who helped with the sick call. I don't really know what his position was but I wasn't really impressed with his professionalism. A Mother brought her baby that looked like she was under a year old to sick call. She waited patiently in line with the others. There were so many. The baby whimpered softly as the Mother gently caressed her in her arms. When I first saw the child my memory went back to the little baby girl my two corpsman friends and I had brought into this world and I remembered hearing her utter her first sound that night in Hue City while the battle raged all around us.

    I gently removed the makeshift bandage the Mother had applied to the head of her child and I saw what looked to me like a shrapnel wound. The Vietnamese man helping wanted to apply a fresh dressing and let her go but I would not allow him to do that. I thought she needed to be seen by a Doctor for further evaluation. I was afraid there was a piece of shrapnel still

Battlefield Faith

lodged in the wound. I quickly informed our Officer in charge that I thought this child needed to be medevaced. He said we could take her to the Vietnamese Hospital in Hue City. I didn't like the sound of that. I really didn't want to return to Hue but the needs of that baby outweighed my own. After treating some of the others we escorted both Mother and baby to our LZ (landing zone) and helped them board the #34 chopper we had flown in on. Then the rest of us boarded the aircraft and we took off north, in the direction of Hue City. We were met by hospital personnel when we landed and they accompanied the Mother with her baby into the hospital. We watched them as they walked away. Our task was complete. I thought we would return to the village to finish up but we got a call while we were airborne and were redirected back to Phu Bai for some reason.

    I was always busy during my days at the Regimental Aid Station. We never knew from one day to the next what we would see or what medical emergency we would experience. I was writing a letter during a slow period once and a little ways into it a Marine came in that needed immediate help. It seems he had injured his finger and needed sutures. And you can see by my letter that I must have taken this wound very nonchalantly. With some of the wounds I had seen and the many Marines I treated this one was a piece of cake. I sewed him up and he was on his way.

6 May 1968
Monday

Dear Mother, Dad, & Family

Well, I thought I'd write you a few lines and let you know I'm doing fine and the Lord is with me.

7 May 1968
Tuesday

Well here it is another day. I had to sew up a guys finger & didn't have time to finish so here I am finishing today.

Its pretty hot out today, but I have a fan. Sick Call is where I work, learning new things every day. I really enjoy my work and the docters teaching us as we go along.

Well, how is everyone there at home? Any new changes up at the church? How has the jubilee choir been singing? Are they still visiting other churches?

I still want to go to see and hope Robert does too.

We're going to have a party tonight. We're going to have pizza, steaks, spare ribs & salad. A couple of cooks are pretty good friends with us so they help us out & we help them out. We have an oven for charcoal. One of the chiefs made it.

> Right now its about 3:35, Tuesday evening and I thirty its going to rain. The weather outside looks like it.
> Well I'll close now but will write again soon. Pray for me!
> Love,
> John

    One of the two Navy Chiefs in our group had built a "Dutch" oven with some concrete he had traded for and was anxious to try it out. This is the only party I experienced in Nam. It kind of put us all in an American frame of mind and reminded us of how things would be when we got home. The food was great. The mood was good and we all dreamed of home.

    The rain in Vietnam is unforgiving. I remember going on patrol and passing through some of the villages during Monsoon season. We would be soaking wet and some of the villagers would peek out at us occasionally and they would be dry. We were issued rain suits once. They were green and made out of some flimsy material. The bush tore them into shreds. The suits were supposed to be water proof. We put them on over our jungle fatigues. After putting on our other gear we mounted the trucks. I found a seat near the tail gate as I usually did and as we meandered down the road I began daydreaming of how my home was so far away. I thought of my family and our home so warm and dry. I thought of my friends and the wonderful times we had together. Then I began to feel wet where I should have been dry. I looked down where the zipper should have been and there was none. The suit didn't have any kind of closure at the crotch and I was getting soaked. The same thing was happening to the other guys. We thought, "Boy, somebody really ripped off the government at our expense!"

Story of the Rifle I found in Nam

    We were on a patrol once again and after walking for a while looking for the "bad guys" we decided to stop for a break. There was a river where we stopped and as I looked over at the bank near the water I saw something sticking up out of the ground. Thinking it might be a booby trap I decided to investigate so I told a couple of the men what I had seen. I thought if it was we needed to find out so no one would be hurt. When we got closer I realized it was a rifle barrel sticking up out of the soft river mud. Again thinking it could be booby trapped I looked around for a rope of some kind. I found one. I was very careful. We talked about what we thought would be the best way to retrieve the rifle and where we would place ourselves if we decided to try the rope.

    We agreed a lasso might work so I made one with the rope and threw the loop at the rifle. It landed on target and I slowly pulled the rifle out of the mud and toward where we were lying. I jiggled the rope and rifle a bit when I started pulling to see if it was booby trapped but it came free from the mud. Then I pulled it closer and when I decided it was safe I pulled it still closer to me. It was not booby trapped and after I removed all of the mud covering it I discovered it was a small M1, 30 caliber carbine. The Vietcong would steal weapons frequently from the ARVN soldiers and they must have lost this one or left it behind for future use against us. I carried the rifle for the rest of my time with Charlie Company but I can't recall using it in Hue. I gave it to a Marine friend when I didn't need it anymore. I guess he too passed it on. I asked once if I could keep it and take it home with me and they said no because it would be considered a recovered American weapon and had to be turned back in.

Battlefield Faith

8 June 1968
Saturday

Dear Mother, Dad & Family,

Just a few lines to let you know I'm doing fine & the Lord is with me. I'm still here in Phu Bai with the 5th Marine Regiment. I have a pretty good job. I'm Master at Arms & Mustering petty officer.

I saw Marshall a couple of days ago. He's looking pretty good. He hasn't changed much.

Here I sit with a fan blowing on me & across the desk & Marshall's out on some hill. He's with 81 mortars where I used to be.

At this time those things were memories. I had a good job now and I was clean and dry. I had plenty of food to eat and it was hot. I had supervisory duties now. I was the leading petty officer just under the Chief corpsman. I had to make all the work schedules and I taught classes to all the new men coming in to our regiment.

Chapter 13

Hanging In There

"During this reporting period the Battalion has worked with the people of Phu Da II. A total of seven homes were destroyed in Phu Da II, and numerous other buildings were in need of roof repairs. The Battalion supported Phu Da II through the village chief with the following materials: 284 sheets of plywood; 240 sheets of plastic (for water proofing); 20 trailer loads of scrap lumber (to be used for fire wood); and 32 wooden 105 ammunition boxes.

The villagers seemed to be quite pleased with the material; the homes that were destroyed consisted of scrap material and c-ration boxes. .."

(This note taken from http://1-5vietnamveterans.org/15-combat-ops/)

After Phu Bai we moved to an area south of Danang called An Hoa. I remember boarding a C130 in full battle gear and upon entering the aircraft we saw no seats but there were several ropes tied across the deck of the plane for us to hold on to. The Marines knew exactly how to board and take their place on the big bird. I was always amazed at the professionalism of these Marines. I was so proud to have served with them. They are experts at what they do and you are indeed privileged if you are accepted by them and permitted to serve with them. As corpsman we also had to be expert at what we did. We took pride in our work and confided in one another whenever time and circumstances would allow us to be together.

1st MARINE DIVISION (REIN), FMF, VIETNAM.
AN HOA (Pronounced AN WA)

Dear Mother, Dad & Family,

I thought I'd write you all & tell you everything is going fine & I am in good health. The Lord is with me and helping me every hour.

Well, I'm not in Phu Bai anymore! I'm now about 23 miles south of Da Nang at an air station. The 5th marines are now here & we have a few Navy Seabees and Air Force personnel.

The chief corpsman is trying to get me out of here on the 5th of September and by the Grace of God I'll be out of here. I have to spend a day or two on Okinawa. They check our gear and we get our uniforms ready to come back to the states —

Battlefield Faith

> Well, tell everyone hello fa me & I'll write again soon.
> Love, John
>
> P.S. Pray fa me
>
> I saw Marshall & he said he has to go on an operation. I told him I'd say a prayer for him. I know God can do anything.

As the introduction to this area denotes, we were not only seeking the enemy to destroy him but we were there to provide relief to the villagers who had been victims of this war. An Hoa proved to be different than the other areas we operated in. I was in a different position here. Now I was working for a Doctor and I was the second highest ranking enlisted man in charge of our sick bay next to our Chief.

We even had a small refrigerator in sick bay where we kept some of our medicines. We were also able to keep some clean, cold water in there. It was great to be able to open that door, feel the cold and enjoy that cold water in the heat of Vietnam.

I remember once we were supported by a troop of Army choppers from the 1st Air Calvary Unit. I walked down to the LZ after they had come back from one of our operations. I noticed some leaves had been snagged by some of the windshield wiper blades. One of the pilots came over and we started a friendly conversation. I asked him about the leaves and he said that they flew low to avoid sniper fire. I was very impressed with these brave men and glad they had come to join us for a while. They complimented our team very well.

1st 3D MARINE DIVISION (REIN), FMF, VIETNAM.

10 August
Saturday

Dear Mother, Dad & Family,

Well, I thought I'd write & let you all know everything is going fine. The Lord is with me & protecting me.

The VC are supposed to be launching another offensive at DaNang & we're (5th Marines) supposed to keep them from it. I'm glad we have a troop of helicopters from 1st Air Cav (Army) here with us. They're a pretty good outfit.

The Doctor, the Chief & myself visited the German Hospital here at An Hoa. It's not very big but it's pretty nice. They have a few Nurses & a woman doctor; also a couple of male technicians.

Well, the Dark Ale Story is on now. It comes on every Saturday.

They have the chapel fixed up for services now. Sunday morning worship, Thursday evening Bible study. I sure will be glad to get home so I can come to our own church.

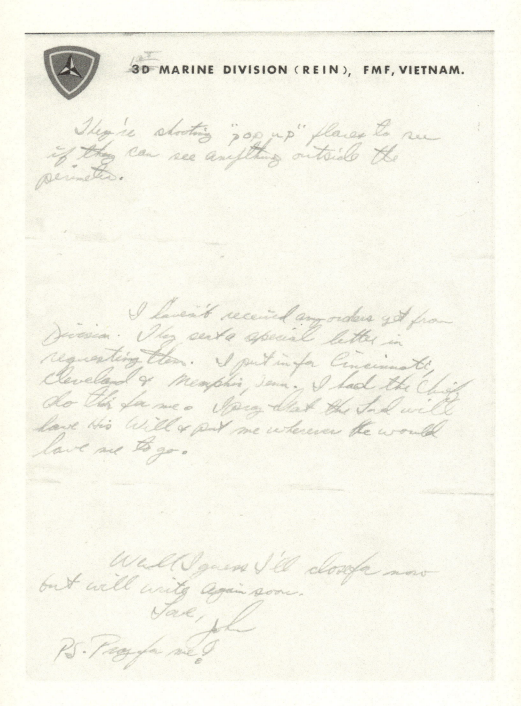

1st 3D MARINE DIVISION (REIN), FMF, VIETNAM.

They're shooting "pop up" flares to see if they can see anything outside the perimeter.

I haven't received any orders yet from Division. They sent a special letter in requesting them. I put in for Cincinnati, Cleveland & Memphis, Tenn. I had the Chief do this for me. I pray that the Lord will have His Will & put me wherever He would have me to go.

Well I guess I'll close for now but will write again soon.
Love,
John
P.S. Pray for me!

Loudermilk

For me, An Hoa had some accommodations I had missed for the past several months. We had a radio in sick bay and I was able to hear the Grand Ole Opry on Saturday nights. We also had a chapel where we could go to church. Once I was able to go with our Doctor and Chief corpsman to visit a German hospital at An Hoa. It was clean and fairly nice but it was small.

I was getting closer to my rotation date. The word was we could request 3 duty stations when we rotated back to the States and we would get one of them. Well, don't ever believe the rumors you hear in the military. I wanted to be stationed close to home but home in 1968 was Cincinnati, Ohio and there weren't too many Navy or Marine Corps Bases near there so I ended up with orders to (drum roll) ---Marine Corps Supply Activity, Philadelphia, Pennsylvania.

30 August 1968
Friday

Dear Mother, Dad & Family,

I thought I'd write you all a few lines to let you know everything is going fine & the Lord is with me.

Well, I got my flight date. I leave Viet Nam on the 9th of Sept. I go to Okinawa from here & stay there anywhere from 48 hrs. to 3 days. This is to get all my gear together and get myself ready for civilization again.

I should be home by the 14th at least. As soon as I get to the states I'll call you all and let you know I'm on my way home.

I'll be glad to get some good food once again. I guess my stomach has forgot what real

> food tastes like. Anything I eat when I get home will be OK as long as it doesn't have rice in it. (Well I'll finish this tomorrow & tell you where I'll be stationed.)
>
> 31 August 1968
>
> Well, I'm getting stationed in Philadelphia, Penn. at the Marine Corps Supply Activity. I'll either work in a dispensary or as a supply man.
>
> Well I guess I'll close for now but will write again soon.
>
> Love,
> John

I was so excited when I got my flight date. My nerves were bad at this time and I asked the Chief if it could be arranged for me to work my way home on a ship. He said he would check it out for me. I really didn't want to fly. I felt I had flown on just about everything in Nam and I wanted to keep my feet on the ground as much as possible. I also wanted to take my time getting home. I wanted to mentally assimilate myself back into "the world", as we called home. It didn't work out though so I gladly accepted the fact that I would fly home. I considered all the positives and thought I'd be united with my family sooner.

At the time I thought Pennsylvania wouldn't be that far from home. It was the next state over from Ohio and maybe I could get a dependable car and drive home whenever I could.

Well, the day had finally arrived and I would take out the year old starched utilities I had been carefully saving to wear on my flight out of here. I would be going home at last! I don't know how I did it but I kept those utilities clean for a year. I can still remember how excited I was when it came time to take them out of my sea bag and put them on. These were my "going home clothes!"

Here I am in my "going home clothes".

I wore my jungle utilities and my "oversize" size 12 narrow boots (they said that was the closest size to a 10 ½ or 11 they had) for a year. Like me they had become bedraggled. Now my uniform and I were clean and prepared for our long waited journey to "the world", as we called it in Nam.

I remember the day I left An Hoa. My cousin, Marshall, came over to the Regimental Aid Station and wished me a safe trip home. It was difficult to leave him there but I knew he would be coming home in a few weeks. After a good handshake and a warm farewell I told Marshall I'd see him at home in a little while. (Marshall did make it home safely). The first time I saw him at home I asked him how it went after I left and he said it was one of the toughest days he ever had.

I walked down to the runway the Seabees had constructed there in our jungle habitat. They did a great job. A small fixed wing aircraft landed with some supplies and outgoing cargo was loaded. I was then told I could board the plane. You entered and exited the plane from the rear.

The plane had a pilot and a co-pilot. There was a small seat behind them for any passengers. The plane was full of cargo. I only had a little room to sit and stow my gear. We had a smooth takeoff and flight toward Danang. As we began to approach the Danang airfield the pilot seemed to feather his engines. The plane dipped slightly. I thought it was a smooth flight. However, I guess they were looking back to see if it frightened me. They looked my way and seemed to smile at each other as we abruptly descended. I thought to myself if you only knew what I have been through. I have flown on #46s, dual prop choppers, fully loaded with heavily equipped Marines, so low to the ocean that the waves almost licked the aircraft. I have had to jump from #34 choppers, where combat ready Marines have been packed into and walked through river mud up to my knees. I have fallen from the sky like a rock and landed in hot LZs with my fellow Marines as the enemy's rounds would zing through one side of the aircraft and out the other. I thought, "This flight is like butter."

The pilot guided the small aircraft down slowly and we landed safely. I can't remember how long I had to wait for my flight out but I do remember getting a thank you card and a pin from the United States Marine Corps for my service to my country and the Corps when I checked out.

The airliner was on the runway. The Soldiers, the Sailors, the Airmen and Marines were standing in line waiting for the call to board. Suddenly the alarm sounded. We all said, "Not now!" We had to leave our positions and scramble for the nearest bunker. We all made it safely. We didn't have to wait long for the all clear though. After a few minutes it was safe to form a line again.

We finally boarded the aircraft, stored our gear and fastened our seat belts. Everyone was anxious to get that party started. We had a very smooth takeoff and once we were high in the air the pilot greeted us and said, "Let's say goodbye to Vietnam!" He tipped his wings and we all shouted, "Yeah!!

I felt relieved and released! The shackles that held me to this place had been shaken off. I was free. Praise God, I could go back to the world, my world. I would see my family soon. The tension and stress of daily survival would cease. We had endured, persevered and we were going home! There were a lot of happy guys on that plane and you could sense the anxiety of

Battlefield Faith

battle was ceasing. The flight wasn't long and soon we landed in Okinawa. An NCO greeted us after we left the plane and we were told if we had any souvenirs we had to turn them in to be checked and we would get them back afterwards. That's the last I saw of my three enemy bayonets I found in Hue City. They also kept my NVA shaving kit with a "Red Star" and the NVA belt and belt buckle with red star. I was very disappointed. Somewhere there is someone telling a story of how he fought hard to get his souvenirs.

    I was glad just to be going home. Thank GOD for giving me life and for giving me life again! GOD gave me life as an infant when I took my first breath and GOD gave me life again when I left Vietnam and returned to my family.

Chapter 14

Home Sweet Home

With exhilarating anticipation I boarded the plane that would be taking me home. We flew out of Okinawa and I remember the happy faces. Everyone on board was in a wonderful mood. We had done our duty and then after a few hours our plane was landing in San Bernardino, California. We disembarked the aircraft and were ushered into a hangar where we were told to assemble. We were met by a senior NCO who gave us a welcome home speech. He then told us we would have to go to the PX and buy some civilian clothes because our uniforms were not popular here. He told us a story of a Marine going home by bus and when he was stepping off of the bus he was shot and killed. He told us of other incidents and said we would not be allowed to leave the base if we did not change our clothes to civilian attire. We looked at one another dumbfounded. We couldn't believe what we were hearing. We all felt like we had done well representing our country on foreign soil. We were proud to be Americans and now we didn't know how to feel after this speech. But the NCO was right as we all found out. What a discouraging welcome home!

We all obeyed orders, bought new civilian clothes, and then we were permitted to leave. We were on our own and had to buy transportation tickets home. Most of the men made their way to the airport. I could not! My nerves were too bad so I got a cab and asked the driver to take me to the Greyhound Bus Station. He dropped me off at the door and I walked in and bought my ticket home then I boarded the bus and rode it across our great and wonderful land.

I thought to myself, "Last week I was in a battle zone and now I was heading home to be with my family in Cincinnati, Ohio". We had moved here from Kentucky when I was a kid. I left the bus at Indianapolis, Indiana then phoned my brother, Robert, to drive there and pick me up. I wanted us to have a one on one visit and catch up on things and I was tired of the bus after my long ride. I remember the first sights of our home as we drove up our street. There were no lookout towers, no concertina wire, no troops, no military vehicles, and no sirens warning of coming danger, no shouts, and no hum of motor vehicles, no clanging of tracked vehicles, no helicopter gunships, and no artillery batteries firing their big guns. There were only the familiar sounds of home that seemed so foreign to me since I had not heard them for over a year.

I had written Robert earlier and had called home just three days prior from California to let my family know I was on the ground. My family had visited a church a few days before I had arrived on American soil and Pastor Troy Davidson's wife came to my Mother and told her that the son she had been praying for would call her in three days. Well, I called in three days!

I had spent three mandatory days in Okinawa before flying to the States. When I finally touched down on my native soil I didn't want to leave it again. My nerves were shot and I couldn't persuade myself to fly the rest of the way home. I had flown very much in Vietnam during the past year and wanted to see my homeland from the window of a Greyhound bus. It took me about three days to get to Indianapolis but I enjoyed the ride. I saw the land. I met some unique people but I never told anyone I had just come home from Vietnam. I remember once the bus stopped somewhere out west to what seemed to me like the side of the road near one small desert town. The driver opened the door and a colorful weather seasoned cowboy got on carrying a saddle. One look at him revealed the genuine article.

My Dad and Mother, brothers and sister were glad to see me and they were relieved I had made it home safely. I was so happy to be home also but there was something within me that words cannot explain. I felt a void in my life, emptiness. My Mother would often say "I was the same" but I was not. No one could have gone through what I had for a year and not changed. I think a lot of people choose to be in denial sometimes. Now and then things that happen to us are difficult to bear or we don't know how to comprehend them.

I was 20 years old. I had been over half way around the world twice. I had fought and served with a US Marine Corps infantry company in a ruthless Southeast Asian war. I had seen many young Marines brutally wounded and I had personally held many of them in my arms as they looked me in the face and took their last breath. They didn't die alone. Our brother Marines and corpsman made sure none of them died alone. They were not left alone. Our duty was to bring them back. We tried with all of our ability to do just that.

So many thoughts seemed to reverberate in my mind as I lay on my bed that first evening. I couldn't get to sleep easily. I heard all of the new "old" noises I hadn't heard in so long. The window was open in my bedroom and I could hear the soothing sound of a gentle breeze rustling the leaves of that giant oak tree just outside. Occasionally I heard a car go up or down the street. I didn't hear any explosions, no small arms firing, no mortar or artillery rounds going off in the distance, no sirens, and no screams of "corpsman". These thoughts began to ease off a bit as I began to realize "I was home!" This was my home. All I could do was to thank God for His Divine Protection and deliverance. Thank God for hearing and answering the prayers of my Mother, my Dad, my brothers, sister, my Pastors, my friends and my prayers. I was home!

When I woke up the next morning as I began to stir in my room there was a tap on my door. As I said, "Come in" I glanced over and I noticed the bedroom door looked as though it was hanging on just one hinge. My Dad walked in followed by my Mother. I said, "Good morning." They replied and asked me if I was alright. I said, "Yes." We then began to talk and Dad said, "We heard you last night." "Did you have a nightmare?" I said, "I don't remember anything. Why?" He then told me he heard some noise and then everything settled down. When he came to check on me this morning he saw that the door was just hanging as we saw it now.

I couldn't remember a thing that happened during the night. I didn't remember waking up. I didn't even remember a dream but I guess I must have had a doozie. This was just the beginning of the many restless nights I would face. Sometimes even now I find I am very restless at night. There's something about the night that reminds me of walking through the darkness to a distant ambush position. I have to make myself stop when I began to think of these things because I can almost hear the deafening sounds of a command detonated mine. I remember seeing the bodies of young Marines being flung through the air and the screams of wounded men yelling for "corpsman!" I try not to remember the smells of war. The scent of gunpowder and bloodshed haunt my memories. (I hate walking through certain parts of the grocery store) There were so many injuries.

The year I returned home Reverend Henry Robertson, a pioneer preacher and seasoned minister recognized I was facing some sort of dilemma resulting from the war. He must have discerned some early PTSD symptoms. He advised me to go to the V. A. Hospital in Cincinnati and get a physical but I did not feel I actually had a problem at this time. I thought if anyone had a problem it wasn't me. I was young. I had survived a war of grueling combat and witnessed horrific battle scenes but I had not attained much wisdom at this point. I could not see myself as I actually was. I just ignored my PTSD symptoms.

After my short leave at home I left to report in to Marine Corps Supply Activity in Philadelphia, PA which was my last duty station. I only had six months remaining on my enlistment and I was eager to get it over.

When I reported in they told me they had no quarters for me and that I would have to go find myself a place to live more or less. I had made E5 (HM2) in Vietnam through a field promotion and because of this the facility had no quarters for E5 and up. We had to find our own living quarters. Oh well, what else was new. Here I was in a strange place meeting new people I had never seen before and who had never seen me. We knew nothing of each other. I had come a long ways and had no place to lay my head. At first I thought what in the world am I going to do now? I had driven my 1960 red Chevy convertible here so I thought I could at least stay in my car if I had to. But one of the other men was renting a room at the YMCA and he thought they might have a vacancy. I went with him after work and was able to rent a room and it became my home until I was discharged in March of 1969.

I drove home for the weekend whenever I could. I think that it was around a fifteen hour trip or so in my car in 1968. I would drive straight through whenever I could. Going home was easy. The trip back to Philly was tougher. I'd start back late Sunday afternoon and drive all night. Sometimes I would get back early enough so that I would have a couple of hours sleep before I had to go to work on Monday morning. Many times I had just enough time to take a shower, get dressed and report for duty. I'd work all day then in the evening I'd eat my supper and crash in my bunk. It was worth it to me because I had been away from my family for so long and I had met Sandy (my future bride) and the miles could not keep me away whenever I had a chance to see her again.

My pay was not enough to live on after having to pay rent. I had to take the subway or bus to work. I had to buy my own food. I was given a small allowance but it was not enough. One day I realized I had to find a supermarket or starve so I went out pounding the Philadelphia pavement to find one. After walking the streets for a while I finally saw a neighborhood store. I went in and browsed a bit. I didn't know much about shopping at this time. I never had to do it before. I ended up buying a few things.

After a while my money ran out and it was a few days before payday. I didn't have a refrigerator or a place to cook any food so whatever I bought had to be non-perishable. I bought potato chips and the like and since it was winter I could sit something on the windowsill just outside my window. I really didn't have a clue on what to buy. This was out of my area of expertise so I ended up buying a jar of "pickled pigs feet" and a loaf of bread and survived on this diet until my discharge. However, sometimes just after payday I would walk several blocks to a small hamburger joint and buy a couple of cheap hamburgers.

It was in Philadelphia that the signs of combat began to surface. A wonderful Jewish lady named Rose Cohen, who worked at the Supply Depot, had evidently observed me on more than one occasion asked me if I had bad dreams about my combat experiences. I brushed her off by saying, "Not too many." I never talked to anyone about my nightmare of 1967-1968. One evening after work I remember walking back to my room at the YMCA when suddenly a helicopter flew over. My heart began to pound and I felt like it would almost explode inside my chest. I began to break out into a cold sweat. I heard the screams of the wounded, the shouts of those in charge, the smell of blood and gunpowder and I immediately threw myself to the pavement at the curb with everyone staring at me. I really felt out of place. I was embarrassed and now my uniform was dirty. I must have looked like a lunatic to the passersby. As the years have gone by I have found that my symptoms increased greatly after age forty. I had symptoms before I left Nam but they became more severe as it seemed my life stresses increased. Sometimes I felt like a wild animal. I either had to fight or take my flight.

During these days I felt the anguish of Job.

Job 7:6-11 *My days are swifter than a weaver's shuttle, and are spent without hope.*

O remember that my life is wind: mine eye shall no more see good. The eye of him that hath seen me shall see me no more: thine eyes are upon me, and I am not. As the cloud is consumed and vanisheth away: so he that

goeth down to the grave shall come up no more. He shall return no more to his house, neither shall his place know him any more.
Therefore I will not refrain my mouth; I will speak in the anguish of my spirit; I will complain in the bitterness of my soul. (KJV)

But this was not the end of Job! He believed in a God of deliverance. As he continued reminiscing about his life he remembered God's promises of hope. The scriptures reveal he did not lose his faith in God.

Job 42:12 *So the LORD blessed the latter end of Job more than his beginning* (KJV)

The time passed slowly. I couldn't wait to get out of the military and go home. I did receive one honor while I was stationed there though. I was presented the Vietnamese Cross of Gallantry, for action in Vietnam, by our Commanding Officer, Major Linneman, as the incoming and outgoing Navy Chief Hospital corpsman witnessed. An article and my picture were placed in the Marine Corps Supply newspaper. I didn't have a ceremony. I didn't even get the medal. But I did receive the honor of the award.

Not long after this I was discharged. I took a lot of emotional baggage home with me in March of 1969. I wish I could have left it behind but it is difficult for someone to experience the heavy combat I was involved in and not have some lingering memories he or she wished they could forget.

I remember when my cousin, Marshall, and I got home after our tour of duty in Vietnam that we wanted to go hunting. We never gave it much thought so we set out to buy some shotgun shells at one of the local stores like the huge ones we have today. We casually walked back to the sporting goods department and approached the clerk at the counter. She asked if she could help us and we explained what we had come for. When we finished talking she just stared at us and said you "boys" are not old enough to buy shotgun shells! We looked bewildered at her response and asked her, "Mam, do you realize where we have spent the last year of our lives? She said, "No!" Then we told her we had been assigned to a US Marine Corps infantry company and were both combat veterans. Marshall even had a Purple Heart medal. We had fired all kinds of weapons and seen fierce combat. We had our military identification cards to prove who we were. She said it didn't matter where we had been or what we had done because the State of Ohio will not allow her to sell us shotgun shells or any other kind of shell because we were not old enough. We looked at each other in perplexity then turned around and left the store flabbergasted and with no shells.

Most of the time I have a difficult time sleeping through the night. Like so many other nights I find things to do until I am so sleepy I have to go to bed. I sleep with three things nearby: my Bible, my Flashlight and my handgun. I had a dog but he is gone. I slept better when he was around but I can't bear the thoughts of getting another pet and watching it die. So I get up frequently. I normally sleep about two hours or so then wake up. I check the house and make sure everything is secure. I check it again and again. Then I go back to bed and struggle to get back to sleep. This is a normal night for me. I'm glad Sandy is a sound sleeper or she wouldn't get any rest either.

I don't drink or do drugs. Once Marty Ising, a wonderful, dedicated VA Counselor, asked me, "John, how is it that you seem to be keeping yourself together after suffering such a high degree of trauma as you have?" The only answer was, "I don't place my trust in medicine or counseling alone. My Battlefield Faith has sustained me. My confidence is in The Lord. He has been a constant companion to me. I place my trust in Him."

Oh yes, I got married in May of 1969 shortly after my discharge. I fell for her the first time I saw her. I went to church with my family while on leave in 1968 and saw a new face in the choir. I thought she was beautiful with her bright eyes and silky, curly long black hair.

When the choir finished their songs she was asked to sing a solo. I watched her as she took her place at the piano and I was floored when she began to play and sing. That's all it took. We were later introduced by a longtime friend at church and the rest is history. Here is our picture in 1968.

Sandy and John in 1968

A few years back Sandy, now my wife, recognized my restlessness and saw I needed a hobby. I had picked the guitar a little bit off and on while growing up. I really never got very good. It was just something that really interested me. My sister-in-law lent me her brother's old guitar when I was in my early teens. The tuning pegs were broken off so I had to tune it with a pair of pliers. I used to listen to a show on the radio out of Cincinnati, Ohio. I think it was WCKY. It was the "Don and Earl" show. They said I could send in 50 cents or so and they would send me a book with the basic guitar chords in it. I saved my lunch money which was 50 cents per day until I had the amount I needed and ordered the book.

    The book arrived one day and I gathered it and the old guitar and began my lessons. I played off and on over the years but gave it up somewhere along the line. I hadn't played the guitar for many years when one day Sandy brought home this old Fender Acoustic she had found at a local pawn shop. It was pretty hard to play at first so I searched and searched for information on how to make it play better. I finally taught myself how to do a setup. I had paid a technician once a large sum of money to fix a guitar for me and it didn't play any better when I got it back so I thought I'd give it a shot. After a few mistakes I figured it out a bit and got the old Fender playing pretty good. I learned how to install a pickup and soon I bought a little amp. I always admired Chet Atkins, Merle Travis and the other fine fingerpickers so my brother in law, Mark Emory, one day hooked me up with the Homespun Tapes website where I could get a VHS tape on how to play the Chet Atkins/Merle Travis Style.

    I'm still working on it. I get frustrated at times but I enjoy playing the guitar. I can get alone just me and my "git" and I feel like it is therapy. Sandy was right. I needed a hobby. I tried hunting but every time I'd get out in the woods I went to war. I had to quit. I tried fishing but I'd get so aggravated especially if I went out in a boat. The boat would usually quit and there I'd sit. So thanks to my little wife I am hooked on the guitar and I really like playing it. I enjoy picking a tune for our seniors every once in a while and at Church and at Christmas. This old guitar is a great contributor to my healing.

    I have found that I can't look back too much. I have to look ahead. I've also learned that people will disappoint me but I can believe in the promises God has given us in His Word. My experiences in the war caused me to feel that we humans were so feeble and breakable but one of the VA Doctors told me one day, "Yes, John, but we are so resilient!" Thanks Doc for that word of wisdom.

Battlefield Faith

I was admitted to the VA around 1993 for PTSD. They had gathered a group of veterans together and wanted us to go through a new program to help veterans like us. I met some real combat vets and I met some real phonies. One Counselor asked my friend and me about a certain patient in our group. We said we see he has a problem but his problem is not like ours. In one of our sessions he said he was a Marine and he was trained to go out alone to set up ambushes. He also said that his weapon of choice was a 30 caliber machine gun.

Once "Rambo" (a name we gave him) said he went out on a mission and hid behind the haystacks. When it was all clear he said he dug a hole on the trail large enough for him to get into. He then crawled into the hole with his "weapon of choice", which he said was a 30 caliber machine gun, and pulled some bamboo and leaves over him. He then claimed he waited for an enemy patrol. When the patrol came by he said he allowed them to pass over him and when the last enemy soldier went by he jumped out of the hole, brushed off the leaves and opened up with his 30 cal. We just sit there and stared at each other in awe. Such is what you may find at the VA. I felt that because of abusers like this it made it difficult for guys with genuine problems to be helped. Some men walked out. Some didn't feel the VA could help them. Some of the men I talked to were genuine. I tried to get them to stay but like so many of us the trust was just not there. It took me and many of the other guys a long time to gain confidence in the system and accept help.

One good thing about the VA is that there are other combat veterans suffering with the same things many of us are. If we could just force ourselves to have a little patience in the beginning, if we would wait for the Doctor or Counselor to see us instead of walking out the door we might find the ray of hope for which we have long searched.

As you read these words I hope you find me as being genuine. Check out my record if you can and you'll find I am for real. Marines and FMF corpsman are invited to our 1st Marine Division Reunion we have annually. If you have been a member of our Division then you are eligible to join us. Check out our website and you may hook up with some friends you haven't seen for a while. I'm like so many combat vets who have had an awful time fitting in anywhere I go. One place I feel at home is with my fellow combat vets and you will too.

Go here: http://www.1stmarinedivisionassociation.org/

Loudermilk

http://1-5vietnamveterans.org/

Around 1997 my cousin, Marshall, called and told me the 1st Marine Division was having a reunion in Cincinnati. He asked if I wanted to go. Marshall had served in Delta Company about the same time I had served with Charlie. He had been wounded but returned to finish up his tour of duty. I wanted to go to see if anyone remembered me and I thought I might see some old friends. I was surprised when so many of the guys did remember me and to my great honor they called me "Doc" after all these years. Several wives of the Marines I had helped greeted me with a thank you kiss on the cheek. I was so humbled.

I know many combat veterans including myself deal with survivor guilt. We agonize over the wonderful men we have known and question why they are gone and we are still here. But I feel we must hang in there. In some way we may be able to bear witness of what we have endured and be instrumental in telling the story of those who have given the ultimate sacrifice. We must look forward through faith and believe even in the harshest circumstances that God never let us down. Our friends reside in a beautiful city where we will all live one day if we keep the faith. We must look around us and visualize how God has blessed us and not go silent and seek to be alone. I don't like crowds either but my wife is a great help to me. She has learned the art of running interference. She is my buffer. God has blessed me in spite of myself and I thank Him for it.

Sandy and I have two wonderful children. Stefanie is a Nurse. Johnny is an Ordained Minister of the Gospel. Stefanie has two hard working children, Grace who is a Phlebotomist and Steven who is finishing up his degree, and one grandchild herself, Grace's son and our great-grandson, Grayson. Johnny and Michelle have four children. Jonathan is an Ordained Minister and his wife Gey and both are serving as missionaries in Thailand as I write. Jared is an Ordained Minister serving in Tennessee. And Jenna and Justin, their twins, are both in advanced learning programs in Kentucky.

Sometimes you may ask yourself, "Has my life made any difference?" Just remember the movie with James Stewart and Donna Reed, "It's a Wonderful Life" and you will see that your life has touched others. Our children and our grandchildren are here because we were spared. Our story can be told because God has granted us more time. The stories of the brave

Battlefield Faith

men who have given their upmost for our country will have their message spoken through us.

Conclusion

I have felt great sorrow. My very soul and Spirit have been challenged. My body has suffered. I have endeavored to persevere in the face of extreme adversity. I lost an incredible amount of weight during the year I spent in Vietnam. I face emotional trials every day of my life now but through all of this I stand on these verses:

Romans 8:37 ..., *in all these things we are more than conquerors through Him that loved us.* (KJV)

Philippians 4:13 *I can do all things through Christ which strengtheneth me.* (KJV)

I am a witness to God's providential care. I am a walking, breathing answer to my Mother's, Grandmother's and the other faithful ones as well as my own prayers. God had a reason for me and others like me to get back home safe. Some of the best men didn't make it. I don't know why. I wanted all of them to make it. All I know is I must "keep on keeping on". God has a plan and we are all part of it. Only someone who has had battlefield experience knows the turmoil that we combat veterans face every day and confront every night. It is difficult to handle alone. Thank God I have an understanding wife that has learned as I have how to recognize these PTSD symptoms and we turn to God's Word and pray for peace. And I remember:

Isaiah 26:3, 4 *Thou wilt keep him in perfect peace, whose mind is stayed on thee: because he trusteth in thee.*
Trust ye in the LORD for ever: for in the LORD JEHOVAH is everlasting strength (KJV)

Battlefield Faith

If you are a combat veteran or someone who has suffered serious trauma in your life and reading this I say to you "Don't give up". Hang in there. There are better days ahead for you. Get help. Don't put it off. You may be like I was. You know you have a problem but you just don't know what it is. You've done more, witnessed more, suffered more, and endured more than anyone should ever have to. You have borne a heavy load. You have done your duty. Now it's time for you to be cared for. Go to the VA, take your DD214 and tell them you'd like to get some help in dealing with the issues you face every day.

https://www.veteranscrisisline.net/

https://suicidepreventionlifeline.org/

Remember,
I'm on your side and I'm praying for you...............

"Doc"

Addendum

Here are some pictures of my Bronze Star Award Ceremony, November 6, 2016. The Mayor of Louisville, Kentucky proclaimed it John Loudermilk Day.

Lieutenant Nick Warr reads the Bronze Star Citation while Major General Richard Huck, John "Doc" Loudermilk, Mrs. Sandy Loudermilk, SSGT John "Mother" Mullan, Marine Gerry Regan look on

Battlefield Faith

Major General Richard Huck Presents Bronze Star Citation to Doc John

Kentucky Lt. Governor Hampton presents Doc John with official Kentucky Colonel and Kentucky Admiral Citations.

Doc John is congratulated by Major General Huck, who was very complimentary of the citation, and all that Doc John did as a U. S. Navy corpsman.

Guests of Honor – 1st Row: Lt. Gov. Hampton, VA Commissioner Henry, Major General and Mrs. Huck and Nick Warr, 2nd Row: Ky. State Representative & Wife, Senator Mitch McConnel Representative & Wife

Doc John receiving kisses from former Miss America and KY VA Commissioner Heather French Henry

Doc John, Sandy and the family and Marine Corps League Guests

The very proud Loudermilk Family and Lt. Governor Jenean Hampton

Detachment Commandant Froehlich cuts the cake.

Missing Marine Table as Tradition Dictates

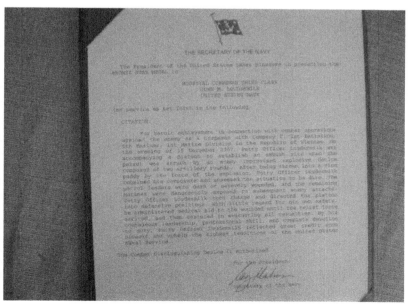

Battlefield Faith

John "Doc" Loudermilk and his beautiful wife Sandy

TO GOD BE THE GLORY..

Numbers 6:24-26
The LORD bless thee, and keep thee:
The LORD make his face shine upon thee, and be gracious unto thee:
The LORD lift up his countenance upon thee, and give thee peace. (KJV)

Philippians 4:7
And the peace of God, which passeth all understanding, shall keep your hearts and minds through Christ Jesus. (KJV)

The End and Amen

Thank you for purchasing my book. If you enjoyed reading it I would greatly appreciate your posting a review at your favorite retailer. Thank you and may God Bless.

About John M. Loudermilk, 1

I was born in Williamsburg, Kentucky. Like many families from the coal mining areas of Appalachia our family relocated north when I was still a youth in order for my Dad to find work. We became country transplants in a big city that offered many opportunities for those brave enough to accept the challenge.

I left school at the age of 17 to join the Navy and I completed my education and received a High School Diploma from the United States Armed Forces Institute in 1966 while stationed in the Philippines. I also completed 2 years of college at Lee College (now Lee University) in Cleveland, Tennessee in the early 70s.

I met my wife, Sandy, when I returned home from Vietnam in 1968. We started dating and were married in May of the next year after I was discharged from the military. We have two children (Stefanie and John 2) six grandchildren (Jonathan (& his wife Gey), Grace, Steven, Jared, Jenna, Justin), and one great grandchild (Grayson).

I have worn the uniform of four of our branches of service. I wore the Navy uniform after I joined the Navy in 1965 and then in 1967 I was assigned duties to the Fifth Marines and was issued a full sea bag of Marine Corps uniforms at Camp Pendleton, California. In the early 70s I joined the Army National Guard while a student at Lee University and was issued Army uniforms. Still a few years later I joined the Air Force National Guard in Louisville, KY where I wore the Air Force uniform. I am proud of all of my service to my country but I am most proud of my duty with the Fifth Marines.

Sandy and I are retired now and attend church where our son, John M. Loudermilk, 2 is our Pastor. And by God's grace I am a Father, Grandfather and Great Grandfather.

I believe in prayer. I believe God hears us when we pray.

1John 5:14, 15 *And this is the confidence that we have in him, that, if we ask any thing according to his will, he heareth us: And if we know that he*

Battlefield Faith

hear us, whatsoever we ask, we know that we have the petitions that we desired of him.

Made in the USA
Monee, IL
11 December 2020